GOING TO SCHOOL

A Dual Memoir

IN BLACK

of Desegregation

AND WHITE

CINDY WASZAK GEARY *and* LAHOMA SMITH ROMOCKI

Torchflame Books
An imprint of Light Messages
Durham, NC

"The events described are always less significant than the impressions they leave on the mind and heart."
—*bell hooks*

"Many things are true at once."
—*Elizabeth Alexander*

"Hearts must change."
—*President Barack Obama*

FOREWORD

Congratulations to Dr. Cynthia Waszak Geary and Dr. LaHoma Smith Romocki for their discourse on *Going to School in Black and White: A Dual Memoir of Desegregation.*

The desegregation of Hillside High School was a tremendous challenge of human growth and intellectual awakening of mind, body, and spirit. Fortunately, the administration, board of education and the parent-teacher-student organization accepted the challenge of embracing the change of human culture and lifestyle. God's wisdom gives us love, faith, hope, joy, peace, patience, kindness, gentleness, and self-control.

The writers of this literary piece are honor graduates of Hillside High School, Durham, N.C., who continue noteworthy contributions to humankind.

—Dr. John H. Lucas, Durham, N.C.

June 29, 2017

John H. Lucas Sr. was named the principal of Hillside High School in 1962 and was there during the events described in this book. He remained as principal until 1985. He went on to become president of Shaw University and was elected to the first school board of the newly merged Durham school systems, serving as its vice chairman. At age 97, he continues to be an active member of the White Rock Baptist Church where he is a Deacon Chair Emeritus and serves on multiple community, state, and national boards. He remains beloved by thousands of Hillside High alumni.

Dr. John H. Lucas, Sr.

PROLOGUE
Why We Wrote This Book

During the North Carolina summer of 1970, the Durham City Schools submitted "The Permanent Plan for Desegregation of City Schools," approved two months later by the N.C. Court of Appeals. The "Plan" altered the school careers of two teenagers who lived across town from each other, 15-year-old Cindy Stock and 13-year-old LaHoma Smith. Both were assigned to schools they never anticipated attending, and eventually, both were brought together to attend the same high school. They became friends, but their friendship did not develop until many years later under very different circumstances.

Cindy, a white student, had just completed her three years at the predominantly white Rogers-Herr Junior High School and, until that summer of 1970, expected to move up to the predominantly white Durham High. LaHoma, a black student, attended the newer of the two predominantly black junior high schools, Shepard Junior High School, as a seventh grader.

The Permanent Plan for Desegregation sent them to different schools than they would have attended otherwise. Cindy was assigned to Hillside High, Durham's historically black high school, and LaHoma was assigned to Whitted Junior High, the other, much older, black junior high school in a well-worn building across town, to be integrated with white students.

Going to School in Black and White is the dual memoir of two students who eventually found themselves at Hillside High School from different sides of a court-ordered racial "balancing act." We are Cindy and LaHoma, and our experiences were the literal embodiment of desegregation policies, situated in a particular time and place. As adults, we have reflected on how these experiences played out on our individual paths. We now share these intertwining personal stories that are part of a bigger story about America, education, and race—and about how the personal relates to the political.

This story runs counter to the usual narrative in that it is a story (at least initially) of integration of white students into black schools. And it is unique because it brings together two perspectives. One perspective is that of a white student who found herself for the first time a part of a racial minority, and the other is that of a black student who had never attended integrated schools and could not understand why she had to leave a school she loved for one she felt was inferior. *Going to School in Black and White* focuses on our junior high and high school experiences but also moves beyond to college, where race and racial integration at our respective universities continued to shape our lives. Through the prism of our current friendship, each of us considers how our school experiences influenced life decisions and how these decisions brought us to similar places.

Memory is subject to bias and distortion when examined through the lens of more recent knowledge. Care has been taken to verify whatever is verifiable through public documents, and some names have been changed to protect the privacy of people we included in our stories. Adolescence is a murky time at best as we sort ourselves out, trying to understand who we are and how we feel about what is going on in our lives. With this in mind, we have been as honest as we could in sharing our experiences and feelings from more than 40 years ago.

ONE

Setting the Stage

LaHoma

I grew up during a time when the integration of the Durham public schools was thought to be the single most important factor in improving the lives of the city's black residents. The idea was simple—if they went to schools with whites, black children would benefit by attending better-resourced schools, and that would lead to more academic opportunities and social mobility as a way to ensure social and economic success. This was the rationale for the struggle in which my parents and most of the adults I knew were engaged.

I moved overseas after college in the late 1970s and lost touch with the day-to-day skirmishes on the front lines of school integration in my hometown. Judging from my experiences and evidence from the people with whom I kept in touch, the integration experiment had been mostly successful.

All my friends had graduated from two- or four-year colleges, attended graduate schools, law schools, and medical schools, and had secured jobs or started their own businesses. I had long convinced myself that integration had benefited all of us, despite my youthful objections. The naysayers had been wrong. Those who dared to believe otherwise appeared to be a dwindling minority.

As newlyweds, my husband and I moved back to the U.S. in 1989 and searched for a place to call home. We looked in the greater Durham area and eventually settled on a small, rural community about 12 miles north of Durham. The reason for not moving back to Durham was largely a financial one: We could afford to buy more house and property in the country. My Yankee-born husband, Tim, was a newcomer to North Carolina, and I thought that it would be fair if we lived in a relatively new community for both of us. Besides that, Tim loves the outdoors, and our new home suited both of us. He had a place to fish and garden, and I relished the large backyard for family cookouts. I reconnected with Durham friends from my youth. Many of them already had children in grade school, but none in high school, and although we talked about a lot of things, I never thought to ask about the school system. In hindsight, I realize we might even have discussed schools, but the subject didn't register in my pre-kids brain. Our conversations were nostalgic reflections of Hillside "back in the day," but they never led me to ask about the Hillside "of today."

So I was speechless when I read an op-ed piece in the News & Observer of Raleigh, the nearby state capital, about the state of public schools in Durham. I brought the article to share with Cindy and our former doctoral advisor, Jane, with whom we had formed a small writing group. I read aloud to them: "Durham schools' student population is now 17 percent white, 25 percent Hispanic, and the rest mostly African American. Seventy-seven percent of the 33,900 students who attend Durham's district schools qualify for a free or reduced price lunch. In some schools, the percentage is more than 80."

The 2015 op-ed described the dismal end-of-year letter grades awarded to the Durham school system. Out of 53 district schools graded, 29 received either a D or F. The article stated that as Durham's district schools' grades had begun a downward slide, "there has been a corresponding increase in the number of high poverty schools and more segregation by race and class." The writer continued: "It's frustrating that the schools are growing poorer even as the city enjoys a boom in restaurants, the arts and downtown real estate. In that paradox, the responsibility can't be put on conservative lawmakers. It reflects the decision of middleclass (white) residents to send their children to charter or private schools…." (1)

"What happened to the grand experiment?" I mumbled to myself and then turned to Jane and Cindy. Everything had worked out OK for me and my friends; had it not worked out well for everyone? What was wrong, and why were white parents moving their children out of the Durham public school system?

I looked over at Cindy, who was shaking her head slowly as she considered my question. Several minutes later, we realized that we had been at the same school, at the same time—during the integration of the Durham public school system. As we peeled back layers of memories and feelings about this pivotal period in our lives, we realized that we were reliving events through different racial filters.

Our reactions brought more questions to the fore as we considered this newly found connection from long ago. Was there something unique about our individual perspectives that was worth exploring? Would we gain greater insight through reliving a shared journey of our experiences? Had my assumptions about the merits of integration been so wrong? We also wanted to make sense of the troubling narrative unfolding about race, class and education in Durham, a narrative that seemed at odds with our own experiences.

Over the past couple of years, Cindy and I have grown closer as we nurtured our budding book project. We learned that we have a great deal in common. We also realized that we were embarking on an ambitious project with immeasurable pitfalls. What if our memories were distorted with the passage of time? We promised each other to stay true to our authentic voices even if they did not always portray events or ourselves in the most flattering light. As we worked through the transitions of inquiry and research, meditation and reflection, awe and abandon to our writing, we revealed stories and shared memories that we thought had long ago faded away.

In the middle of our discussions about if and how we wanted to share our stories, I attended my 40th high school reunion, talked to old classmates and teachers, and even got a hug from Dr. Lucas, the high school principal at Hillside when both Cindy and I were students. I told a few of them about the book project and received overwhelming interest and promises to purchase a copy once it was published. But more important, their opinions validated my own, regardless of whether they were black or white. We all seemed to believe that the experiment had worked and that we had indeed been its greatest beneficiaries. Former classmates fondly remembered our time together, with many having made tremendous sacrifices to come to the weekend event. Others had used the occasion to visit elderly parents or siblings and other family members still living in the area. Many, like me, lived in Durham or nearby. The reunion of more than 120 alumni and their families, both black and white, reinforced my resolve to finish the project.

Together, Cindy and I tell our stories of integration in the context of our lives in our different communities. What appears here is the result of reaching far back into our memories to put to paper the feelings that these experiences elicited. This book, I hope, will contribute to the local, state and national discourse on whether there is inherent value in requiring children from different racial and ethnic backgrounds to attend integrated schools together.

Cindy

The civil rights movement of the 20th century took place on many stages, but arguably one of the most important was public education. The intention of the Brown v. Board of Education decision of 1954 was to bring equality to the education of black children whose segregation from white students was recognized as counterproductive to that goal. Sending black and white children to the same schools was part of a socialization process as well, with the expectation that children of different races would learn to get along with each other, even if their parents had not. Enforcement of Brown came at a slower pace than "with all deliberate speed" might suggest, but it did eventually come in the late 1960s and early 1970s, after much resistance from white school boards and parents. Racial equality required court-ordered school redistricting and buses, and it required black parents and white parents who were willing to support their children as they ventured into new geographic and social territory. Equality also required children who trusted adults to protect them.

My schooling was part of this social-change experiment as it played out in Durham, North Carolina, in the 1970s. What difference did it make? I imagine there are as many answers to this question as there were children in school. In this book, LaHoma and I tell our stories of integration that converge with and diverge from each other in telling ways. LaHoma and I did not know each other while we attended the same school. We were two years apart in age and had gone to different junior high schools, having lived in separate parts of a racially segregated city. We did meet each other some 15 years later when we worked for the same organization in Durham doing global public health work. We still did not know each other well because we worked in different departments, and LaHoma eventually left to return to school for a Ph.D.

LaHoma and I remained in overlapping networks of friends and colleagues; in 2014 we found ourselves part of the writing group she described above with our mutual friend and mentor. During a meeting of this group, over a mushroom and artichoke frittata at a local bakery, LaHoma and I discovered that we both were students at Hillside High School the year she was a sophomore and I was a senior. A torrent of memories took over our discussion that day, and we realized we had a story to tell, made richer by our individual perspectives. In our conversation about the op-ed piece she brought in, we realized we also were similarly concerned about the way Durham schools (and schools everywhere) have reverted to racial segregation because of a combination of white flight and the loss of a court mandate to maintain racial integration.

The resegregation of schools in Durham that LaHoma writes about reflects a reality across the country. The percentages of black students enrolled in schools in which the student population is 91-100 percent minority (often referred to as 'hypersegregation') ranged in 2011 from 34 percent in the South and West to 51 percent in the Northeast, reflecting substantial increases since 1991(2). Learning about this turn of events woke us up to the startling realization that though we had been among the students whose school lives were altered by court decisions to promote racial equality, we had not actually given much further thought to what this meant to us. Nor had we paid close attention to what had happened in the schools since we left high school.

Our immediate reaction was that this reversal in policy and its effects felt wrong to us. We wrote this book to explore our own experiences and find out what was good and helpful to us from them—as people who believe in racial equality and as citizens who believe that our government has a role in ensuring equal access to education for everyone. We wanted to find out if we had idealized the value of our experiences and/or if they had made some difference in our lives. It was important for us to do this together, to bring stories from our separate racial identities. We wrote separately but read each other's work frequently and then talked to each other about what we learned from each other.

Our motivation for writing this book evolved as we wrote and shared. At first, we wanted to tell stories that we thought reflected a particular place and time, stories about our coming of age that might resonate with others. Later, we began to see the value for each of us in the conversations we were having as these memories surfaced. Some of what we were telling each other was surprising, and some of it was confirming. A lot of it was just fun—reliving high school memories several decades removed. It was our common history and our willingness to listen to each other's stories with our hearts that created our true friendship with each other. Examining our past has been revelatory; this examination has kicked up a lot of questions for us, too. We have done much soul-searching for answers, and we are still not sure about some of them. But we are committed to the continuing conversation.

Writing this book has been a gift to me, a time to remember what we had not thought about for so long—what my poet friend Jaki Shelton Green calls "remembering what you remember"—and to understand it in the context of what we know now and what we are still learning. Writing together has doubled the gift for me, not only transforming an acquaintanceship into a strong friendship but also giving us a chance to understand this time in our lives from another's perspective in a safe and trusting collaboration.

TWO

In the Beginning Was "The Letter"

LaHoma

The summer of 1970 was a long and agonizing one for me. There had been talk—rumors—that the Durham City School System was going to make changes and that some students were going to be reassigned to go to schools with "the Whites." The grownups in my life didn't talk about it with me much, but I could hear them talking about "it" to each other and how "it" was going to change everything. I didn't like the uncertainty I heard in their voices, but I tried not to dwell on it too much. I was secretly hoping that the changes they were talking about were not really going to affect me, that I would just be able to continue to go to the best school in Durham with my friends.

I had spent my first year of junior high school at Shepard, a relatively new school for black students. The school was named after Dr. James E. Shepard, the president and first chancellor of what is now called North Carolina Central University. Shepard was THE place to be if you were a gifted black young person in Durham, as I believed myself to be. Shepard was located between the vibrant and prosperous commercial district on Fayetteville Street and the residential area of Alston Avenue and close to prominent black churches, including Mt. Zion Baptist Church, White Rock Baptist and St. Joseph AME Zion. Close by Shepard were also the Rosewood and Emory Woods neighborhoods, communities for upper middle class and affluent blacks where, if you lived there, in my young mind, your father was probably a doctor or a lawyer or worked at North Carolina Mutual Life Insurance Company or Mechanics and Farmers Bank, the most prominent black-owned businesses in Durham. These businesses had given Durham its reputation as the home of the country's Black Wall Street.

My family lived in the opposite direction, in Southeast Durham only a block or two from McDougald Terrace and Lincoln Apartments, a community of blue-collar and lower middle-, working-class families. Most of my friends came from these neighborhoods.

I believed that the best teachers taught at Shepard, and the school certainly had the resources and support of the surrounding black communities. Shepard was also the place where all my best friends were. I could not imagine what good would be accomplished if I were forced to go to another school to be with strangers, even if they were white. What were "they" thinking? My godmother, Mrs. Smith, an English teacher at Shepard, explained to me that officials were trying to make things better for Negro children, but I couldn't understand what was wrong with the ways things were. I longed for nothing; I lacked nothing. My parents, my extended family, my godparents, my neighbors and my church family provided everything I needed. I had always been encouraged to excel and was shielded from the era's negative depictions of Negroes. I was an avid reader, and the library in McDougald Terrace was one of my favorite places to spend my afternoons, walking slowly among the shelves, careful not to miss the latest books to arrive.

My father worked as a medical technician, a full-time, state employee at Memorial Hospital in Chapel Hill, but he always had two part-time jobs in addition to his main one. My mother, a licensed practical nurse (LPN) at Duke Hospital, was also an excellent seamstress who made all my clothes and took in repairs to "make ends meet." We owned our own home with a big backyard in which to play. How could going to school with white kids make the world any better for me?

Life in seventh grade at Shepard Junior High School was idyllic. I was a good student, full of potential—and, yes, college bound. Everybody told me so. I knew I was smart—but so were a lot of us, and we were all treated as if we were "somebody" and expected to do well. Even though many of us came from families with modest incomes, our principal, Mr. Schooler, teachers and parents worked hard to provide us with the resources we needed. It is only now that I can acknowledge that perhaps our parents and teachers saw what we didn't see—that we didn't have the same access to books, materials, supplies, and other resources in our schools that the white students had in their schools. These adults yearned for access to those resources for us.

We were so proud of the school field trip to Nags Head organized for all the seventh graders. Our teachers and families had raised the money so we could all go regardless of where we lived or what our daddies did for a living. The teachers had emphasized how important it was to get us out of the classroom so we could see North Carolina, not just read about it in textbooks. So we traveled, two busloads of 12- and 13-year-old Negro children to what I now understand is exclusive beach property. We visited the inland sand dunes and Kitty Hawk, and I learned about the Wright Brothers and the importance of aviation. The bus ride home was long, but I was thrilled to be sitting next to Derek, the cute boy whom my best friend, Skeeter, and I both had a crush on. I was secure in feeling that I was where I belonged.

I tried to think practically about the logistics of a move to a new school. How would I get there? I had to walk to Shepard because of my parents' work schedules. But it was fun. Almost every day a group of us would walk the two to three miles home along busy Alston Avenue to the side streets of Rosewood. Now who would I walk to school with?

The arrival of "the letter" confirmed my worst fears. My mom says I brought the notice home from school that "it" was coming soon, but we didn't receive official notification until early August. The knowledge that the unwanted school re-assignment was coming hovered over me like a pesky fly, ruining that summer for me.

I read through the short form letter several times, but it still didn't make sense. I could no longer go to Shepard Junior High, just because I lived on the wrong side of Plum Street. Friends on the same street but on the other side of the arbitrary line drawn through the heart of McDougald Terrace could remain at

Shepard. If you lived on the "wrong" side of the street, as I came to see it, you were assigned to Whitted and now were forced to trek to the end of the earth to go to school. "It is so dumb," I thought, "this whole integration plan." The adults in my life tried to console me, but I refused to oblige them. Nothing they could say would convince me that this decision had not ruined my life. I did have a few friends who also were reassigned to Whitted. We called one another, cried, and commiserated about our fate—why did this have to happen to us, why couldn't we go to the school we wanted to go to, and why were some of our friends allowed to stay but we weren't?

I was not at all curious about what it would be like to go to school with white students, and I had no feelings of apprehension about their presence or absence in my life. I just couldn't believe that race was the reason I needed to change schools. "I have been around white kids before," I reminded my mom. "Remember, Camp Mary Atkinson—the Girl Scouts camp in Johnston County?"

My mother, in early attempts to expose me to white people, had packed me up for two weeks of tent camping when I was in fourth, fifth, and sixth grades. More often than not, I was the only black girl there. I hold mostly positive memories from camp, and the young, friendly camp counselors really protected me. Some of the little white campers, curious, wanted to touch my hair and feel my skin to see "if it was real." But mostly, I learned to swim, hike, canoe, and cook over a campfire, all skills that have served me well throughout my adult life. My positive interactions with the Girl Scouts left me with the impression that I knew everything I needed to know about white people. Why did I have to be the one to leave the school, friends, and teachers I loved?

My resentment toward Whitted Junior High School grew as the first day of school loomed. Whitted was in an older school building that had originally been Hillside Park High School, Durham's first high school for African-Americans. Whitted School, as I came to learn, began in 1887, when Durham established the first black grade school in North Carolina. In 1922 older students moved into a new building, Hillside Park High School on Umstead Street, named for the public, all-black park next to it. By 1949, the city school board decided to make a swap and moved the high school, along with its name, to the newer J. A. Whitted Elementary school building near what is now N.C. Central University. The elementary pupils were moved to the building on Umstead Street, keeping the Whitted name for the elementary school, but changing the building name. Later, Whitted Elementary became Whitted Junior High (3). Whitted was also near many black-owned businesses, including the Imperial Barbershop, the *Carolina Times* newspaper, and the Stanford L. Warren library.

Though I later grew to appreciate the historical importance of the area, at that time I didn't know or care much about it. I did know and care that in 1970, Whitted was not close to my house or my friends. I justified my anger by putting down the neighborhood surrounding Whitted. As a black kid, I knew which white areas in Durham to avoid; likewise, I knew where my friends lived. And I didn't know a lot of black kids who lived over on that side. I just felt more comfortable walking through my side of town.

Tensions ran high those first few weeks of school that fall, as black students newly assigned to Whitted from around the city joined the black students from that neighborhood. The new students were indignant at being forced into this new arrangement, and the neighborhood students felt that their turf was being invaded. Either way, the anxiety levels were palpable as we all tried to adjust to our new circumstances.

And then of course, we had to get used to going to school with the white students.

Cindy

A new court-ordered desegregation plan in the works for the 1970-71 school year was about to wreak havoc on my middle school dreams of attending Durham High School. The alternative to Durham High would be Hillside High, a historically black high school, which I had never seen and knew nothing about. I would be a racial minority for the first time in my life.

My three consecutive years at Rogers-Herr Junior High—from seventh to ninth grades—were an unusual time of geographic stability for me. Before then, I had moved to new cities and changed schools almost every year since the first grade because of my father's job as a telephone installer. I had rarely let myself imagine where I'd be going to school the next year, much less in three years, but this stay in Durham had lulled me into feelings of certainty and continuity. Now, external forces were about to change my plans.

Junior high school had been a difficult transition for me. The social environment at Rogers-Herr was more complicated than what I had known in any of the elementary schools I had attended; social class determined so much of social life—something I had rarely thought about before starting to school there. This uncharted territory and my painful shyness made it rough going for a while, though I eventually found a group of friends. By the end of ninth grade, I finally felt comfortable in my space and was imagining my life at Durham High—hanging out with my friends, joining a few clubs, going to basketball games and dances, and maybe finding a boyfriend among the upperclassmen.

* * *

During the spring semester of ninth grade, however, it became apparent that something was going on that could disrupt my plans. A new, much-discussed desegregation policy might require a new school assignment. Everything was in process, and there was no way to know who would be going where. Anxiety ran high, but no specific information was available. The real tension, among the grownups at least, was about race and what was about to change and for whom.

A citywide hearing at the beginning of summer vacation gave Durham parents their first glimpse of where their children might be assigned to go to school in the fall. The map from the first draft plan indicated that I would be assigned to Hillside High School. Neither I nor my parents attended this meeting, but the map was printed in the Durham Morning Herald the next day with a report on the meeting reflecting the unhappiness expressed by both black parents and white parents and other adults who had been there. Representatives from black community organizations spoke of concerns about the proposed closing of an elementary school in a black neighborhood. Representatives of white supremacy groups such as the Ku Klux Klan and the Citizens Council spoke about fears for their children's safety and anticipated violence. White parents wanted to understand better the reason for the plan and the process undertaken by the school board to meet the district court's requirement (4).

At the end of the meeting, school board members promised they would take another look at the plan to see how they might address some specific issues. So, though this first map provided a pretty strong indication of my school assignment, the matter was not completely settled, and there was some hope I still might go to Durham High.

This uncertainty continued until the Durham City School Board sent out "the letter" to each student on August 7, only a few weeks before school was to start. The notices we received were form letters with blanks to be filled in: "Your child, _____, has been assigned for the 1970-71 school year to _____ School. Yours very truly, Lew W. Hannen, Superintendent, Durham City Schools." The letter I nervously retrieved from my front-porch mailbox late that summer had "Cynthia Claire Stock" and "Hillside High" handwritten in green ink in the two blank spaces. I was disappointed but not surprised.

This letter was the final word on the matter—I would not be going to Durham High School. I did not feel angry nor especially unhappy about the fact that it was Hillside per se. I just felt disappointment and that teenage sense of injustice about not getting to go where I wanted to go. All of my close junior high school friends—Judith, Beth, Brenda, Jen, Chris, and Lynn—also were assigned to Hillside. We took some comfort that we all would be going to Hillside together.

* * *

At age 15, my friends and I were not civil-rights activists, nor were we overtly racist. Talk about our new school assignment was not couched in racial terms, though we must have felt somewhat nervous about being the new white kids (and lowly sophomores on top of that!) in a previously all-black school. None of my friends left the city school system or went to a private school because of the assignment. We knew that some students from our school—but not my friends—were going to go to prep school because of this assignment plan, but they were children of wealthier parents—lawyers and doctors and businessmen—who did not figure into my world view.

My friends and I knew that black schools were not as nice— not as well-maintained and did not have the same kinds of equipment or educational materials as those that were mostly white—and we realized that this policy was an attempt to fix this inequity. I am sure we wanted to be part of the solution, even if we did not discuss this aloud. But we still had feelings of regret, frustration, and anxiety about the school board's decisions.

* * *

My parents and their friends thought it was unfair and wrong that, to avoid participating in the desegregation plan, some parents moved their families out of the school system or sent their children to prep schools or the "Christian" academies supported by the "Christian Councils" with what we perceived as thinly veiled associations with the Ku Klux Klan. My working-class parents and their friends believed that people should do what the government asked them to do. They also believed in public education, so there was no doubt that our family would comply with the new assignments.

My parents' sense of duty notwithstanding, they were not exactly happy about my going to Hillside, either. Some of my mother's concerns (and they were always more her concerns than those of my father) were not any different from those she would have had about my transitioning to any high school from junior high. Any high school would have been a bigger school, farther from home, and would have meant being around older students with whom I could get into more trouble. But, added to this list now were worries about how unknown everything about Hillside was to us and about how being a racial minority might affect my school experience.

Their primary fear was about my safety. Was Hillside in a safe neighborhood? Could they let me stay after school to participate in extracurricular activities? Could racial tensions at school flare up and erupt into violence? My parents never spoke this last question out loud as some of the white parents had at the public meeting in June, but in light of televised news stories from previous summers about crime and rioting in poor black neighborhoods, I knew this was part of their fear.

My parents and I were also worried about the quality of my education. Though it embarrasses me to say this now, there was a perception that black teachers would not be as good as white teachers, and that they would not hold us to the same high academic standards as those in the predominantly white schools in other districts. I was a serious student, and academics were important to me. I worried that I would fall behind my white peers at other schools whom I would be competing with for college admission in three years.

* * *

On my first day of school at Hillside—and every school day for the next three years—my mother drove me and my friend and neighbor, Judith, to school in the morning and picked us up in the afternoon. Though "busing" became synonymous with desegregation in the 1970s, busing was not an essential feature of the Durham plan for junior high or senior high school students. I could have gotten vouchers to take the city bus—a trip that would have required changing buses in downtown Durham—but my parents vetoed that plan (and I didn't argue with them) because of their worries about safety and the time it would have taken me to get to and from school.

I had never even seen the Hillside school building before "the letter" brought me to my first day of classes there. It was no farther from where we lived than Durham High, but it was in a part of town we never had any reason to visit. When we drove up that first day, we saw a big brick building with lots of students, black and white but mostly black, standing around outside waiting for the bell to ring. The building was not very different in appearance from Durham High School, other than possibly being a little older. If you walked through it while it was empty of students, I doubt there would be anything about it that would have made you think, "This is the black high school." Even if you looked from the front steps out at the houses that bordered Hillside's campus, you might wonder which middle-class neighborhood this was and be surprised you had not seen it before.

That first muggy September morning at Hillside, my mother marked our arrival at my new school with her usual lump-in-the-throat, tear-in-the-eye goodbye, and a series of "behave yourself," "be safe," "stay away from trouble" admonitions. I was well practiced in being at a new school, and whatever her reservations about the whole situation were, she was sure I would be all right; I'm sure I thought so, too. Not because I was especially outgoing or self-confident. On the contrary, it was because I was shy and did not want to stand out—I was happy to go unnoticed and fit in and do what high school students do, whatever that turned out to be. I stepped out of our blue Pontiac that morning focused on finding my way into this new and different world.

LaHoma Smith in seventh grade and Cindy Waszak in ninth grade.
Photos courtesy of Shepard Yearbook, 1969-70 and Rogers-Herr Yearbook, 1969-70

THREE

Growing Up Black in Durham
Before Desegregation

LaHoma

I was born in Durham—delivered at Lincoln Hospital on Fayetteville Street, eight blocks from our house. Almost all Negro children needing to be birthed in Durham and surrounding areas were born in Lincoln Hospital. Lincoln was initially financed by the Duke family, and it was commonly believed they provided the money to ensure that white Southerners would be protected from diseases that might be contracted from their Negro cooks and maids. So even though my mother had been working as an LPN at Duke Hospital for several years, she could not give birth to me there. Duke did not open its doors to an integrated patient population until many years later. Duke Hospital also had black janitors, orderlies, technicians, and cooks in the cafeteria. Black employees, yes; black patients, no.

The day I was born, my mother drove herself to the hospital because my father was already at work in Chapel Hill, and it was impossible to get word to him that she was in labor. He learned of my birth when he got home later that evening. I spent my first night home from the hospital at the home of my godparents, John O. and Mary H. Smith. The Smiths, no blood relation, have cared for and looked after my parents and me all my life.

* * *

My mother, Jessie, met Mrs. Smith in 1948 at Hawley High School in Creedmoor, North Carolina—approximately one mile from where I live today. My mother was a student, and Mrs. Smith was the cute, poised, young, substitute teacher, who, according to my mother, didn't take any monkey business from her pupils. She was always impeccably dressed and feminine, belying the depth of her intellect and force of her opinions.

My mother, who had grown up on a farm and labored in tobacco fields as a sharecropper all her young life, longed to become a nurse, but there were no nursing schools for colored girls in that rural area. If she wanted to become a nurse, she would have to move to the big city of Durham. However, the culture of the late 1940s did not usually permit or make it easy for single young Negro women to live independently. So my grandmother implored the worldly Mrs. Smith (who had made her home two blocks from North Carolina Central University in a neighborhood of other intellectually gifted Negro educators) to let my mother stay with her while she attended nursing school. After she and her husband, Mr. Smith, discussed the request, they agreed to allow my mother to rent a room while she completed her schooling as part of the first classes of Negro women to become LPNs at Duke Hospital. Fifty years later, Duke would honor the living members of that group in a ceremony and dinner for their significant roles as "Trailblazers" in Duke's history.

* * *

One day in early March 1950, my mother began her usual routine, checking in on the new patients and emptying bedpans. These were still the early days of introducing the young Negro nurses to the all-white patient population. Sometimes the patients expressed their displeasure at having these colored girls enter their room or assist with their hygienic care. So it happened on this early spring morning that a particularly unsatisfied white man had berated Mom for getting too close to him when she tried to remove his bed pan full of urine. Apologizing for upsetting him, she turned to get out of the room as quickly as she could, trying to avoid his hate-filled rant.

In her haste, she didn't notice the oversize hospital bed being steered down the hall by a young male orderly (who would today be referred to as a medical technician). The two collided, and Mom spilled urine all over him. She apologized to the as-yet-unknown man, tears flowing, and kneeled to pick up the pan. She looked up again to seek forgiveness from the person she had run into. She later recounted that she thought that this was the worst day of her life.

Luckily, she told me, there wasn't a patient on the bed. But that wasn't the only thing that changed her fortunes that day. As she looked at the young guy trying to assess the damage to his clothes and himself, she saw that he didn't seem angry. In fact, he was kind of amused. He started laughing, and "Boy," my mother recalled, "was he good looking—a Negro Clark Gable, mustache and all." We have lots of photos of Adolphus, my daddy. She wasn't lying about his looks. The rest of the fairy-tale romance happened quickly. Courtship, love, and then marriage six months later. She was 21; he was 23. Unable to afford a big wedding, they got married in the living room of the Smiths' house. I came along seven years later.

Although they had managed to save enough to put a down payment on a new house on Plum Street, my young parents were still living paycheck-to-paycheck, and they did not have heat in their new home. They eventually brought me to the 1,400-square foot, three-bedroom, one-bath rancher at the intersection of Plum and Lawson Street in Southeast Durham. It was an all-Negro neighborhood of working-class families that had first broken ground there in the early 1950s. My parents were one of the first families to buy a house in the new development. Both with regular jobs, my parents were able to take out a $35,000 mortgage for their little house with the dirt driveway.

* * *

My mother had two failed pregnancies before my arrival. She tried once again after me, but to no avail, so by the age of 3, I had been raised in a household as an only child with a lot of doting adults looking after me. About that time, however, my aunt and her husband were going through an ugly separation. She had also just given birth to her 10th child. I was too young to know exactly what was going on, but the aftermath of this turmoil resulted in the sudden appearance in our household of my cousin, and now brother, Rudy.

Rudy was about 2 years old, a scrawny little guy who was probably just as confused as I was about this new living arrangement and separation from his nine brothers and sisters. I doubt my mother and her sisters fully understood the impact of what they decided to do, but there is no doubt that family came first, and as I became more aware, I respected their decision to keep their sister's children together in the family. We are bound forever as cousin siblings.

* * *

Over the years, Rudy and I had been in most of the houses on the first block of Plum Street for one reason or another. We knew everyone on the 700 block of Plum Street and many people on Sima, Lawson, Bernice, and Bacon streets nearby. Boys and girls played together on the corners and in the streets, and we knew each other by name; we knew their siblings' and parents' names, too. They were mostly two-parent families— families such as the Thorpes (whose son invited us to his birthday parties only to beat us up), the Fields, the Marables, the Bostons, the Roysters, the Davises. All the fathers would cut grass on Saturday mornings in the contest for most beautiful yard. They shared conversations on front lawns and across driveways about clipping hedges and bushes, and trimming weeds around the sidewalks that provided easy access from one end of the street to the other.

Our immediate next-door neighbors were the Longs, who ran a florist shop. Next to them was Mr. Long's elderly mother, Ms. Minnie. One day I was out in my yard playing, and Ms. Minnie called me over.

"Honey child," she said. "I hear you doing real good in school."

I did not have to think long to know where she had heard that. There were no secrets among the adults in my life, and my good grades were a source of pride for my parents.

"Yes ma'am," I confirmed.

"Well, come over here a minute; I got something I want you to do for me."

So I ran over to her house because she always had a treat, something sugary to give me, and I was a willing subject. Fifth-grade report cards had just come out, and I was hoping she had some sweet potato pie for one smart little girl. I climbed the steps to her screened porch where she kept an eye over the neighborhood. Ms. Minnie was our "neighborhood watch" before that phrase was coined.

I opened the door and waited for her to hand me something deliciously sweet, usually a piece of cake or pie in a brown paper bag—but she didn't give whatever it was to me right away.

"Do you know how to write?" she asked.

I could not tell whether she was serious.

"Yes ma'am." Of course I knew how to write, I thought to myself; who doesn't know how to write?

Miss Minnie said, "I need you to write a letter to a friend of mine who is in a rest home and I probably won't be able to see her soon. Can you do that?"

"Yes ma'am, I sure can," I replied. I noticed that she already had a few sheets of stationery lying beside her chair.

"Take this paper, and let's see how you do."

So I sat down and wrote the first of many letters that summer until Ms. Minnie died. At first I thought that Ms. Minnie, who my Mom tells me was in her 70s then, was too old to write letters, but it became increasingly obvious that Ms. Minnie could not read. I later learned (but not from Ms. Minnie—she had too much pride) that they did not teach black girls to read when she was growing up, and the responsibilities of working and raising a family surpassed any personal ambitions to learn how to read or write.

Ms. Minnie would feign supervision of my work to see if I was writing down everything she told me, but I realized that she was admiring my neat cursive writing on her beautiful sheets of paper. She would smile and give her approval, "Yes, it looks all right," before I could seal and address the envelope.

We fell into a routine. Ms. Minnie would call out to me when she saw me in the yard, as she had that first time, and I would go over to write letters to her family and friends. In the letters she described her health and her church activities, and she commented on the weather. She slowly paced herself to make sure she included all the highlights of her daily existence on Plum Street.

Once in a while, Ms. Minnie would reach for a foil-wrapped bag. She would take a little pinch and shove it into her mouth. As she pondered the next line or waited for me to read what she had already dictated, she would shift her body to the left to spit out a little black juice from her snuff-filled lips. She dabbed at the corner of her mouth with the handkerchief lying across her lap. I didn't like the odor from the spittle, but I got used to it. Besides, Ms. Minnie always paid me for my letter writing—usually 25 cents, or whatever coins she had in her change purse. And 25 cents could buy a lot of candy and comic books in 1968.

* * *

Two blocks over from my house was McDougald Terrace, one of several all-black housing projects in Durham. I spent a lot of time there because my favorite babysitters were the Prince sisters. My mother loved and trusted them. My brother and I would go there after school and wait until my father came home to pick us up. There were always lots of kids to play with and never a lack of fun things to do and places to explore. McDougald Terrace is where I learned a lot of important facts of life, including the truth about Santa Claus. Did I really believe that big fat white guy in a red suit was messing around at night, going from house to house in our neighborhoods? Spoken in those plain words, their logic was hard to argue with.

The residents of Plum Street and McDougald Terrace were not very different from each other, and any conceivable differences were not easily discernible. I didn't see or feel a distinction. To the contrary, there was a strong sense of community, one established by the proximity of our domiciles. We also were part of the larger racial superstructure of these neighborhoods that effectively segregated our daily existence from white Durham through the schools we attended, the churches we prayed in, the stores where we shopped, and the social and civic activities in which we were engaged. Black factory workers and police officers, black janitors and custodians lived next door to black teachers and preachers. We were all members of the separate racial cocoons that divided Durham.

* * *

One of the points of pride on Plum Street was College View Nursery School—today it would be called a preschool. College View was a private preschool for "those black children destined for greatness," as Ms. Alston, the founder, and the parents, family and friends who invested their money to send us there would say. My brother and I both attended CVN, which competed with Scarborough Nursery for the best and most promising young black children in Durham.

Many of the children at College View were from my neighborhood, but children of the black teachers and small business owners and professionals from other parts of Durham came, too. Ms. Alston was known as a strict disciplinarian with high standards of academic preparation and conduct for her 3-, 4-, and 5-year-old college-bound protégés. We were introduced to basic concepts of reading, writing, and arithmetic. We also prepared theater performances for our parents, who shared in the costs for costumes and stage props, and who helped finance our day trips around town to black-owned businesses and professionals.

Ms. Alston, typical of most black adults, believed in the Old Testament's stricture "spare the rod, spoil the child," and the rod was not spared on my behalf. Ironically, if I complained or even mentioned to my parents that I had been punished, they would thank Ms. Alston for correcting my breach of conduct and then take me home to discipline me again. As a quick learner, I tried to keep these episodes to a minimum. Ms. Alston never had too many problems with me. Respecting adults and their rules served me well throughout primary and secondary school days.

Corporal punishment, or physical punishment for bad behavior, was the norm in many black homes and schools when I was growing up in Durham. I learned later through academic literature and reflections with friends that this was not as common a practice in many white families. Some social psychologists have posited that these punishment behaviors were institutionalized in black communities as a way to instill fear of authorities and to protect their children from straying from accepted rules of behavior (5). The best way to ensure that their children would be safe from Jim Crow laws, attitudes and dispositions, both written and unwritten codes of conduct prevalent throughout the South, was to make sure that we were aware of how to obey rules and what would happen to us if we didn't obey them. My friends and I serve as witnesses of the application of this theory. Ms. Alston was the second (my parents were the first) of my many teachers who would continue to reinforce this code of conduct.

* * *

Preschool now conquered, I was ready to move to my next educational challenge—first grade. But I needed new school dresses—not pre-school play clothes. Because this was such a special occasion, my mother said she would buy, not sew, my new clothes. We also bought pencils, paper, erasers, and a book bag to hold all the supplies that my mother was sure I needed. Mom took me to school that first day seemingly without a second thought. The teacher gave me a bright smile, asked my name and had me stand on a scale to measure my height and weight. She told me to find a seat.

I looked around for a familiar face from College View, but seeing none, I just stood there, not wanting to make a mistake with this first big decision of elementary school. I stood there for a little too long, and I heard the teacher repeat herself, "Sit down please." As I finally moved toward an empty chair, a girl looked up and smiled at me. So I sat down and smiled back at her. Angela, or Skeeter as I would learn to call her, and I became fast friends and are still friends today.

After that first day, I walked to school from my house almost every day. I would meet my friends on the street corner or walk down the hill one block to meet others before we crossed a little bridge, then climbed up another hill through a wooded lot until we reached the baseball field on the edge of Burton Elementary. We climbed a long set of stairs until we reached the main schoolyard. This took five minutes on the way to school (if you ran) or an hour on the way home, as we often would chat, play, and chase one another, especially when we got to the wooded lot full of places to explore and hide.

Ms. Ollie was also a reliable babysitter for my brother and me. She lived on the same street as Burton School, so I would walk with a different group of friends to her house on the days she watched us. Her house bordered the wooded area and playground in the neighborhood. There was also the neighborhood recreation center next door to Burton that offered afterschool activities, summer camps, dances, and sports competitions. Everything that I needed in my young world those days was within walking distance of my house.

My sheltered existence at Burton belied the turmoil that was bubbling throughout the Durham public school system. While I worked hard for good grades, played with friends, joined the safety patrol, and enjoyed the freedom to walk to and from schools, the corner store and library, angry voices were insisting on equal access for colored children to the schools beyond the confines of our neighborhoods.

One year before I began elementary school, the Wheeler v. Board of Education lawsuit outlined the general characteristics and challenges of our de facto segregated school system. It concluded that the practices of the Durham School Board were discriminatory, forcing children to attend same-race schools when better schools with more resources were closer to their homes.

As a result of the court decision resulting from these lawsuits in 1961, a couple of Negro children were allowed to attend their neighborhood schools. This debate never affected me because Burton was so close—I could see the school grounds from my front porch, so my parents would never have considered my going to a school in a white neighborhood just to integrate or even to benefit from a supposedly better school. Life was good. Besides, I was a star student at Burton, and I had excellent teachers who encouraged me. I didn't realize or care that we didn't have the resources of the white schools. We seemed to have what we needed. If the teachers or parents thought differently, we didn't know about it.

Even though some Negro children were allowed to attend white schools, the Durham public school system did little to encourage racial integration on a large scale. During these early elementary school years, nothing changed for me. I never saw any white students. One of the ways that the Durham school system sought to keep the status quo of separate but equal was to build more schools in the rapidly growing Negro parts of the city.

So in 1968, a new elementary school was built in my neighborhood, named for R.N. Harris, the first black member of the Durham City Council and the first black man on the Durham City School Board (6). The letter I received in the summer of 1970 mandating that I move from one junior high school to another to achieve integration was really my second such letter from the Durham public school system. I received the first in 1968. I was not allowed to finish my sixth-grade and final year at Burton, but was ordered to move to R.N. Harris, the new elementary school for Negro children, located two blocks from Durham Technical Community College. Now I had to walk three times as far to school every day, but still there were no white students.

* * *

Going to church was a big part of my weekly family life, and it was not unusual to find me at church two to three times a week. My parents were dedicated churchgoers, and there was never a conversation about NOT going to church. It was the norm, the rule, just as natural as drinking sweet iced tea on a hot day.

We had Bible study on Wednesday nights. Thursday night was youth choir night, and Sundays were devoted to Sunday school and worship service. Many Sunday afternoons, we would also have singing programs and observances to mark special occasions. We attended Mount Zion Baptist Church on Fayetteville Street, down one block from North Carolina Central University's present-day student union. It was a joyful place to be, with lots of families from surrounding areas and McDougald Terrace. My parents were very active in the church through choir, ushering, deacon duties, and seasonal activities—Easter egg hunt, Christmas recital. My brother and I were always busy at church.

Once church was over, we would return home to Sunday dinner, with family and friends stopping by to chat, visit, and rejuvenate before the new week. Mr. Smith (husband of my godmother) and Mr. Alston (the vice principal at Hillside High School and not related to my nursery school teacher) were two regular Sunday visitors. They never ate dinner, but they would sit around the table laughing and talking with the family.

Each summer, my mother would find out about all the Vacation Bible schools for churches in our area, and we would attend all of them. Classes were usually brief, divided by the ages of the children, and there was lots of socializing and outdoor playtime, along with a snack. My parents also sent me to Sunday school conferences, where I learned to memorize and recite Bible verses, pray, and sing glory to God.

I never resented attending church regularly, because in addition to pleasing my parents, it was also a great place to meet boys. The lack of reliable telephone communication, especially the cost for calling outside our exchange area, inhibited any budding romance, but it was fun in the moment. Besides, church proved to be a fertile place to feed my needs on so many levels, spiritually and physically. I spent much time building friendships, socializing and flirting with boys, sharing and fellowshipping with neighbors over plates of Southern fried chicken and other home-cooked favorites. I honed my oral skills, reciting Bible verses, memorizing my lines for the Christmas or Easter programs, and participating in regular Bible study discussion groups. I served on the youth usher board. I sang in the choir, and so did my parents and brother. Not a single talent was wasted or opportunity overlooked to praise the Lord in my household. To this day, I cannot understand anyone who ever claims to be bored. I've never had a boring day in my life.

* * *

My father worked two jobs at a time for most of my formative years, as did most of the black men I knew. In addition to his weekday job, he also had a job cleaning or cooking on the weekend, or helping to move the white doctors at the hospital into their new residences. If he did not have a second job to go to on a Saturday, he could be found in the garden in our backyard, a holdover from his youth growing up in rural Caswell County,

N.C., where his family owned hundreds of acres and raised tobacco, chickens, pigs and cattle. Dad was always growing something or coming home with something that somebody else had grown, fished, hunted or slaughtered. My dad's brothers had kept the family place in Pelham and made a good living from the bounty of their expansive farmland. Every visit to my uncles resulted in a return trip with a trunk full of seasonal vegetables, pecans and, of course, meat from a fresh hog kill or their fully stocked freezer.

Even though Dad moved away from Pelham and the family farm as soon as he finished high school, the hard-learned habits of his childhood never left him. As soon as warm weather appeared, Dad would start preparing, tilling the soil, and planning his garden. Living on that corner house in Durham, he made the backyard his canvas, plotting where to plant the tomatoes, string beans, and cucumbers. He eventually outgrew our quarter-acre backyard and started renting small plots to grow fresh vegetables, which he and my mother would can and pickle for the winter months. I learned to love fresh tomato and cucumber sandwiches, to shuck corn, and to snap green beans—although it would take many years before I acquired a taste for his beets and summer squash.

My parents tried to figure out where Rudy's strengths were by enrolling him in one activity, then another. They bought him a saxophone, which stayed locked in the case. He seemed uninterested in academics or athletics. But eventually he found God's gift to him—his beautiful baritone singing voice—which he has used to delight church audiences in and around Durham and neighboring states as a member of the "New Generation" singers. Under the leadership of Oren Marsh, one of the most talented pianists in the area, they offered a spiritually uplifting performance. They were young black men and women who booked Sunday afternoon gospel singing assignments, and all of them were as talented as the groups who were more nationally recognized. Everyone thought they would hit it big one day. Although they always seemed to be on the verge, it never happened, and the group disbanded after five years.

Today, Rudy has a beautiful daughter, who has married and has a son. He has maintained a strong relationship with his biological brothers and sisters, my cousins, and despite the nontraditional family arrangement, our relationship has always been a source of pride for all of us. My female cousins, Ella and Machael, Rudy's sisters, are still my closest confidants.

My large and extended family included my maternal grandmother, aunts, uncles, and cousins who grounded me in love and tradition. Since I was blessed and cursed to have both of my parents come from farming families, I was destined to learn something about gardening despite my protests that I was a city girl.

My mother, now a city girl too, still felt it her duty to help out the family farming during the summers. Using her vacation days, she would take my brother and me to the country for harvest time. My grandma Mozella (short for Moses Ella); my aunts, Ruth, Frances, and Hazel; uncle Berry Lee, and cousins Larry and Little Joe would "pick 'bacca" for white landowners all over Granville and Vance counties in central North Carolina.

And you were never too young to be out in the fields—even if you couldn't pick the tobacco. The older kids who got tired (usually after about 20 minutes) had to look after the younger ones who were too little. We would get up early before it got too hot and work through the morning, then take a break and work through early afternoon until somebody—usually my grandma—decided that we had worked long enough for that day. Homemade biscuits and a piece of smoked meat or tablespoon of sorghum molasses, packed in brown paper bags, made a hearty lunch. After a long morning working out in the sun, those sandwiches were the best food in the world. My mama's sisters were fast workers, too. Wearing large-brimmed straw hats, they labored rapidly through the tobacco fields, filling up the wooden bins. We children often ran down the path to the edge of the property to fill pails and bring back the coldest drinking water you ever want to drink for the adults to let run down their parched throats. Outhouses near the fields provided relief when we needed to go. We always traveled in pairs to the outhouses—to make sure no one accidentally fell in.

Even if we were too little to take the leaves off the stalk, we found all kinds of other ways to amuse ourselves. We picked bugs and caterpillars off the tobacco, and when we had collected enough of them, we would hold a grand funeral—complete with memorized Bible verses, hymns, and eulogies for the dearly departed. To top off the day—if we had been good—Grandma would allow us to jump on top of the horse-drawn sleds headed back to the barn while the men would climb the rafters to string up the tobacco for drying. For the trip back to the house, we put towels on the car seats to protect them from our clothes, sticky with the sweet-smelling tar from the tobacco mingled with the sweat from the day's activities. Bucket baths, dinner, and cold watermelon capped off a full day of summer fun.

My family, neighborhood, school, and church were all important pieces of my evolving identity, and there was a tight network of other people in whom my parents entrusted the care of my brother and me when they were not around. Adjoining our backyard was the house of Mr. and Mrs. Conaway. Mr.

Conaway was a big, burly, guy with a broad smile and deep voice that shook the room every time he spoke.

"Hi, Mr. Bill!" I would call whenever I visited, which was often, since his wife, "Ms. Thelma," was a frequent caretaker for my brother and me on the weekends. Both the Conaways worked for the tobacco factory, putting in long, hard days. Most of Mr. Bill's second jobs were in the restaurant business, and he was a great soul-food cook—collard greens in fatback, pigs' feet, black-eyed peas, cornbread—all cooked the right way—with lots of grease. He also owned dogs that he kept in a fence between his property and ours. My mother always complained about those barking dogs, but it was just accepted as one of his quirky ways, with nothing you could do about it. Many evenings I heard him at the fence, throwing scraps of food into the dog pen, encouraging them to bark at any trespassers, thieves, and unwanted visitors.

Ms. Thelma was always beautifully coifed, with her hair pressed and shining with Bergamot hair conditioner. She loved her hats and matching purses and was always buying things via the mail. She'd show me her Sears Roebuck catalog from which she had ordered underwear, stockings or a dress. I never understood the appeal of shopping by mail or even today's modern equivalent of Amazon and e-commerce. But her habit kind of makes sense to me now—first, because she didn't drive, and second, the use of catalogs reduced her need to interact with unwelcoming white retail establishments. Most of her grocery shopping was done at our corner store, which carried all the items that Mr. Bill loved to cook. Ms. Thelma often sent me to pick up items they needed, with a few pennies to buy something for myself. Ms. Thelma was not much of a cook herself, but she loved sweets and was another lady who indulged my sweet tooth without question.

Two people with the most lasting impact on my life were my godparents, John O. and Mary H. Smith, the same couple whose home had been the site for my parents' wedding. Mr. Smith, a pipe-smoking, peanut eating, no-nonsense math teacher, taught in the Durham city schools most of his life. He taught at Hillside High many years and then at North Carolina Central University until he retired. Mr. Smith visited our home every week. He and my father would unwind from the previous week and prepare for the new one.

Mrs. Smith had moved from Hawley Middle School to become a highly regarded English teacher at Shepard Junior High many years before being reassigned to Rogers-Herr as part of efforts to integrate the Durham School system in 1970. The Smiths were a steady presence in my early life—and just as determined as my parents were that I would succeed. Both of their children, Nathaniel and Joyce, were proud college graduates. The Smiths showered us with educational gifts and books, usually with Afro-centric themes, for every birthday, Christmas or when I received some special recognition. I once received a set of playing cards with famous authors such as Walt Whitman on the cover so that I could remember them for English lit class—because, as Mrs. Smith said, I needed to be well-rounded and know "their history" as well as "our history."

I was surprised they could find these books with black images because I never saw them in our library books or textbooks at school. I think Mrs. Smith got tired of my re-reading *Heidi, Pippi Longstocking, Tom Sawyer,* and *Huckleberry Finn,* my favorites. By the end of sixth-grade year, the Smiths had saved enough money to purchase a complete encyclopedia for us. It was an amazing collection especially designed for African Americans, with photos of prominent blacks all through. I treasured those books because I knew they cost a lot, and they reinforced the Smiths' confidence that I would excel in my studies. Under the watchful eyes of my parents, the Smiths, my neighbors, my family, and other adults in my social circle, I was loved, safe, and protected. What else did I need?

LaHoma Smith (back row, second from right)
at College View Nursery.

FOUR

My White World Before Hillside

Cindy

At dusk one evening in November 1966, with all our belongings packed in our new Chevrolet Bel Air, my family drove into Durham, North Carolina, for the first time. I was 11 years old, and my brother Greg was 6. We had driven up from Florida, where we had lived in Bradenton, Sarasota and St. Petersburg for most of my elementary school experience.

We, as a family, had two immediate impressions of Durham.

First, the street layout was completely incomprehensible— particularly after living (most recently) in St. Petersburg, where the whole city was a grid of avenues going one way and streets going another, numbered in ascending and descending order. Our second impression was there were a lot of black people— more than I had ever seen at one time.

The Durham we settled in, however, was white Durham. We quickly learned where we were supposed to live and go to church and school and to shop. There were no Jim Crow signs (please…that was in the '50s, and this was the '60s!) to tell us these things, but the color lines were evident enough. We were not looking for them; we were not consciously segregating ourselves; we were just finding our place. Our initial racial disorientation soon wore off, and we did not think about it much because it made little difference in our everyday lives. It took us much longer to figure out the tangle of streets and roads to get us to the places where we needed to go.

* * *

I started elementary school in Bradenton, Florida, in 1961, but before that my family had already moved dozens of times, mostly in the Southeast, but also (briefly) in West Virginia (where I was born), Ohio, Texas, and upstate New York. My father installed telephone equipment in one-story square brick box buildings that no one ever notices, equipment that connected telephone lines across the towns where we lived; moving frequently was part of the job. In the six years I was in elementary school, I went to eight different schools, mostly in Florida and North Carolina. My elementary schools were all white except for one or two in Florida, where a few black children were in my classes. I did not see black children outside of school, but my family was so transient that I rarely saw any classmates, except for those at church or in my neighborhood.

One memory of a formative event from this time that now shames me happened on the playground in the third or fourth grade in one of the schools where there were black children. We played one of two games on our concrete playground at recess; one was foursquare, and one was tetherball. The day of this memory I was playing foursquare, a game in which four people each stand inside their individual squares and bounce balls in each other's squares following prescribed rules. Anyone who makes an error is out, everyone moves up to the next square, and the next person in line goes into the first square. My classmates and I spent most of our time waiting in line. To amuse ourselves, someone decided to start observing the racial composition of the four people playing each game, using the words "chocolate" and "vanilla" to note the races represented. There were only white kids doing this.

I went along with this to be cool with my peers. The black girls playing with us were rightly upset about this, and they told on us after recess. My white teacher (they were all white at this school) called us out in front of the class for this bad behavior. I am glad she did; I was duly embarrassed.

Part of the effect, though, was to make me feel that "seeing race" was somehow wrong. So for a long time after this (decades perhaps), I pretended that I did not notice a person's race. I would not mention a person's race when recounting stories to family and friends—and I would resist when others asked for that information by saying I didn't remember. Of course, I remembered, but I thought when my parents or friends asked whether someone was white or black, they were doing so to make assumptions about their behavior on the basis of race. By my reasoning, the asking of the question was a display of prejudice and, therefore, wrong. I had transformed my initial humiliation because of my playground behavior into feelings of moral superiority on the issue of race.

After we moved to North Carolina and I heard people in North Carolina discussing school integration, I thought all that was nothing new to me. I thought my experiences in Florida made me a little more knowledgeable and possibly more principled (having learned my lesson) than my peers in North Carolina. I was wrong, of course.

* * *

We always rented the houses we lived in, and our first home in Durham was out in the county near the airport in a small rural community. The school in that area was an all white, kindergarten through eighth grade, very rural elementary school. In the sixth grade at this school, I enjoyed a brief period of notoriety being the "new girl from Florida." I enjoyed the attention, though I imagined myself more sophisticated than my classmates, who all had strong Southern accents and whom I thus considered rednecks. (I have since embraced my Southernness, however, and love nothing so much as a particular type of strong Southern accent.) We attended a very small Southern Baptist church nearby, and my friends there were school friends as well.

At the end of the school year, our landlord wanted his house back, so we moved to another rented house in Durham, but across town, making it necessary to begin again in a new school and a new church. Though the distance may have been only 10 miles from our first house, the new neighborhood felt like another planet. Instead of being out in the country, we were now "in town," closer to Duke University, in a very middle-class neighborhood a few blocks from the highway connecting Durham to Chapel Hill.

We lived our lives within a relatively small geographic radius. We were a few miles from a shopping center where there were a grocery store, a dime store, and a pharmacy, as well as a theater,

GOING TO SCHOOL IN BLACK AND WHITE

where I was to see many movies that informed my adolescence over the next six years. The shopping center was an easy bike ride from my house and a favorite place to meet friends. The YMCA was also close by, as was a tiny drive-through we called "The Cow Store" because of the nearly life-size cow replica on top. My mother got her hair done at the nearby beauty shop. We walked to the Kwik Mart for frozen sodas in summertime.

Yates Baptist Church and right next to it, my new school, Rogers-Herr Junior High School, were both walking distance from our house. Rogers-Herr, named for two beloved, never-married white Durham female schoolteachers, opened its doors just months after I moved to town, as I was entering the seventh grade.

In 1967 (and until 1992), there were two school systems in Durham, one for the county and one for the city. The county schools were much whiter than the city schools. The elementary school I had gone to when I first got to Durham was a county school. Within the city system I had moved to, however, de facto school segregation reflected the racially segregated housing in the city. City schools were either predominantly white or predominantly black, and I lived in a white neighborhood. The school I went to was predominantly white.

When Rogers-Herr opened in 1967, "freedom of choice" was a passive racial desegregation policy, allowing black children to enroll in any school they wished; Rogers-Herr was built to serve several white neighborhoods, but black children could attend if they wanted to, or more precisely if their parents wanted them to. Looking back at my yearbooks for the 1967-68 school year, I see only 27 black students out of 297 pictured. One black teacher taught music; no cheerleaders were black, although a few black students played sports, and a few were in the band or the booster club. The only other black people in the yearbook were the custodians and cafeteria workers.

The parents of the few black students were mostly professionals, professors at North Carolina Central University. All the black students had attended predominantly black elementary schools before coming to Rogers-Herr and were good students.

One might argue that the small number of black students who chose to attend out-of-district schools supported the claim that most black children did not want to go to white schools. But it was not just the policy that made attendance at Rogers-Herr by black students possible. My black peers in junior high school had parents who were able to get them to school and provide the emotional support to get them through difficulties they experienced being in a nearly all white school. Most black children in the city school system did not have such resources. I was, and most white people were, oblivious to these realities.

* * *

Being a white child among white children, I did not have to think about race when at school. To me, it was much more important to understand what it meant to be "popular." Being a new girl kept me out of the running for being popular in this school, but I knew the coveted status was about more than having been there awhile. I knew how to be the new girl—this was the ninth school in which I had been a (if not, the) new girl. I was quiet; I did not get into trouble; I made good grades. Though I was shy about meeting new people when we moved to a new place, eventually, I had felt as much a part of what was going on as anyone else.

Something was different at this school, though, something that the wearing off of my new girl status was not going to change. That difference was class-consciousness and my loss of innocence about the difference between the lives of the "haves" and the "have-nots." I had not experienced this awareness at any other school. I knew some people were better off than others, but I had always been in schools and churches with children whose families lived more or less like mine, and I was able to participate without worry. My family lived modestly but wanted for nothing beyond what we could afford. Education was the more important metric by which my family measured success.

But in this new school, it was different, and it wasn't just about money. Not all the children of wealthy parents were popular—none of the Jewish kids or the black kids whose parents had money were as readily incorporated into the popular core group as were the blonder, WASP-ier kids. Popular students came from a group I stereotyped as families that belonged to country clubs.

Popularity was established and maintained by conformity to style and behavioral rules. The popular kids continually curated these styles and rules, so this information was part of what separated those popular kids from all others. At the most superficial level, this closely held information manifested as what clothes to wear. I had never heard of Villager or Capezio clothes before junior high school, or even any other name-brand fashion—my mother had made nearly all my clothes.

I realized only certain people could be friends with each other. Only popular students became class officers or first-string on school sports teams or cheerleaders or got lead roles in the school plays. For me, not having been exposed to this cult of popularity in elementary school (as had most of my non-popular peers at Rogers-Herr, I would later find out), my entry into junior high school was disorienting and disheartening. My parents were oblivious to the social landscape that confused and rejected me, and they could not help me navigate it. I see now that this sensitization to class privileges generated my sympathy for other ways in which people might feel they were seen and treated as "the other."

* * *

Cotillion clearly defined my "outsiderness" and its attendant misery. Cotillion was a once-a-month social dancing activity that children joined in sixth grade and continued through seventh grade. Children had to be invited, and parents had to pay. Because I was new, I had not been invited, and I assumed that my mother either didn't know about it or thought we could not afford it. Not only the most popular kids participated in Cotillion, so it might have been possible for me, but I never asked my parents because we knew we shouldn't ask for things we couldn't afford. I assumed I would be putting my parents in an awkward position, so I did not ask.

Once or twice a month that year, many of my classmates anticipated the upcoming Cotillion, went to the dance, and then talked about everything that went on there for the next week—what everyone wore, who danced with whom and who had either increased or decreased their social attractiveness as a result. I may have been better off by not being there, as I would not have had the right clothes or known how to dodge the social minefield that Cotillion would have been for me. But I was a lonely girl on those Friday nights.

* * *

My mother's working at Rogers-Herr two of the three years I was there further reduced any hope I might have had of popularity. I knew of no other mothers who worked. My mother had never worked outside our house before I started junior high school, but with both my brother and me in school, she became the cafeteria manager at my school. Before she was married, she had managed the school lunch program in (what is now) Eden, North Carolina. So she was well qualified even if it had been a while since she had a professional job. She was excited to be the first cafeteria manager in a modern kitchen with all new equipment (including a $10,000 dishwasher!).

To my embarrassment, everyone knew that my mother was responsible for the school's lunches—always a source of derision, whatever the quality. Mother tried to get children to eat yogurt and whole wheat bread before those were popular ideas. I bore up under my peers' moans and groans as best I could.

Mother liked her staff—a white cashier and both black and white kitchen workers. She became friends with the cashier and also was close to one of the black kitchen workers. Managing the cafeteria was difficult, though. In a time when few other (white) mothers had jobs, there was no expectation that a father might help at home. I always had household chores even when Mother was not working, but my contributions were not enough to make much of a difference. After a year, she decided being a working mother was not a good idea.

Mother must have thought the trouble she had finding work/life balance was because of the particular job as cafeteria manager, because she spent the next year taking correspondence courses so she could renew her teaching certificate and go back to work as a teacher instead. She had been a home economics teacher before she married, but she came to my school to teach seventh-grade math and science the year I was in ninth grade.

My mother "the teacher" was even worse for my popularity status than my mother "the cafeteria manager." Apparently Mother expected the same kind of compliant classroom behavior she had experienced in the 1950s from her (all female) high school home economics students, and she was not prepared for the discipline challenges she faced in the junior high classroom. Although I pretended not to hear, kids often said mean things about her. On the other hand, some of Mother's friends were my favorite teachers, and I enjoyed their attention because they were her friends. Teaching wasn't any easier for a working mom than being a cafeteria manager had been, however, so she quit teaching at the end of the year. To my relief, she showed no interest in finding a way to come with me to high school.

Eventually, I made friends with some girls who had been around longer than I, who had similar backgrounds to mine and lived in similar neighborhoods. Judith became my closest friend in junior high and high school and was my eventual roommate in college. She lived just a couple of blocks from my house; we saw each other after school almost every day. Judith was sweet, shy, and petite. She cared about a lot of the same things I did—boys, clothes, making good grades. She was more athletic and outgoing than I was. She had lived in Durham all her life. We both had younger brothers in elementary school. Our mothers became friends.

In the fall of seventh grade, Beth, the daughter of a friend of Mother's, invited me to a church retreat (her church, not mine). Beth's mother bribed her to go by offering her the opportunity to bring a friend. I was grateful to be invited. Beth and I were both shy, and we were glad to have each other's company that cold, autumn weekend. Beth, Judith and I became part of a small circle of friends that included Chris, Jen, and Lynn. We remained close at Rogers-Herr and later, Hillside.

I learned there was little room for moving out of one's social station. With the help of my new friends, I soon figured out my place and what was possible for someone with my status: academic achievement, booster club, drama club, school plays (chorus and tech, not speaking parts), and intramural sports. I also learned what was not possible: cheerleading, class offices, the leads in the plays, and, for boys, sports teams. I kept my aspirations within bounds.

None of my friends in junior high school were black. I certainly talked to my black classmates during the school day, and we were in clubs together, but there was little or no socializing outside of school. I did not consciously avoid being friends with black students or consciously make an effort to do so. We were just in different social spaces. They lived in a different part of town and went to different churches, and their parents were not friends of our parents. There just seemed to be no interface between us, other than in the classroom.

Until a discussion in high school, I had no idea of difficulties the black students had experienced at our junior high school just because they were black. When I noted with some sympathy during this discussion that it had not been so comfortable as a non-popular white girl in junior high school either, one of these black peers said: "Oh, that's right. I remember you were part of that crowd that was not so popular." Even after the changes that being at Hillside had wrought within me, it hurt my feelings a bit that she had noticed.

Luckily for me, I found a place outside of school with more acceptance and less social hierarchy—my church. I was raised as a Southern Baptist, the denomination of my mother's upbringing (though not my father's—he had not gone to church as a child), and church is what grounded us wherever we lived. Church was the center of my mother's social life, and church was where I always knew adults were paying attention to me and cared about me. In those days, churches were rarely integrated, and mine was all white (except for the janitor, who was an employee but not a member of our church).

Yates Baptist Church was close to where we lived and next door to Rogers-Herr. Besides our house and school, church was where I spent most of my time. In addition to being at all worship services (Sunday morning, Sunday night, and Wednesday prayer meetings), I was a member of the youth choir and in other youth activities.

Because of geography and local politics, I had school friends and church friends, with little overlap. Both my school and my church were less than a mile from the line that separated the Durham city and county school systems. Most children who had grown up in my church lived on the other side of the boundary.

When parts of the county became annexed to the city, they were not always also incorporated into the city school system. Newly annexed neighborhoods were allowed to decide which system they wanted to join. Usually, they decided to stay in the county system, effectively maintaining the county's relative whiteness and the city system's greater blackness. Before we moved to Durham, votes to merge the two systems had always failed. Racism played a part, but so did the fear that a unified system would mean an increase in the county's tax rates.

* * *

All my friends at church lived close to me but went to county schools and had very different school lives than mine. My church friends also were from working or middle-class families and had similar educational aspirations. My school friends also lived close to me but attended different churches, so there was little mixing of the two groups. I learned early to compartmentalize my friends by school and church. Within both these places, my friends were pretty much each other's best friends, intensifying a disconnection for me between these two groups. My compartmentalization contributed to a sense of myself that I did not share with others—it was a secret self that knew the whole of my life and relationships but kept that whole to myself.

* * *

The whiteness of both my junior high school and my church meant that I had little interaction with black people in Durham before I went to Hillside. My rather abstract views on race were informed, in addition to my shaming experience in elementary school, by my religious upbringing and my interpretation of Jesus' command to love your neighbor. I was confused about why my church was still all white and why there was no effort to include black people. Although overtly racist remarks rarely were uttered in our church, few spoke about supporting civil rights efforts. The young youth minister, Steve, did encourage our youth group to question this gap between Jesus' teachings and church reality and to consider how we should live our lives within the context of our faith and our community. The formation of my racial consciousness as an ethical issue took place mainly in this space.

* * *

What I learned in my family about how to live in the world and treat other people influenced my racial attitudes. My father, Rudy, was born in Davenport, Iowa, in 1922 to German immigrant parents and grew up working to help his large family of three sisters and three brothers make ends meet. He was a free spirit without tight parental oversight, so when he wasn't on his paper route or some other job, he spent as much time as he was able swimming in the Mississippi River and playing basketball with his friends. After he graduated from high school, he was a census-taker and a bus ticket agent and eventually joined the Merchant Marines during World War II. After the war, he began work installing telephone equipment, a job that required frequent moves around the country.

My mother, Norma, went to college, a rare privilege for a girl born in rural Appalachia in 1924, but made possible through the sacrificial support of her parents and a scholarship from Berea College in Kentucky. After graduating, she taught home economics and then ran a school lunch program, both jobs in a small town in North Carolina. My father's job brought him to this same small town, and there he met my mother at a bridge party. Mother left this town and her career to marry my father and follow him and his job around the country.

My parents both had strong "no nonsense" values, formed in part by growing up during the Great Depression. My mother's childhood experiences were rural and religious, and my father's were urban and secular, but both had grown up in big families where it was necessary to pitch in to ensure everyone had enough food and clothing. Both of their families valued education for boys and girls, although for Daddy's family this meant finishing high school and for Mother's it meant going to college. My father, however, started saving for my college education before I was born. I never questioned that I would go to college.

Both my parents were frugal, and savings were valued more than possessions. Daddy was a member of a labor union, and that union ensured him wages adequate to live modestly, clothe and feed his family, and send his children to college. My parents believed in the American promise of a level playing field at birth, and they taught my brother and me to be honest and to do the right thing even if it was not popular. We were not encouraged to question institutional authority—or to complain.

Our frequent moves around the country had a strange liberalizing effect in the midst of what may sound like an otherwise boring middle-class lifestyle. What we learned that was liberating was that more than one way of being is possible in the world. My parents were more tolerant of the diversity of human experience as a result. My father had seen a lot of the world as he traveled as a Merchant Marine, and my mother was always interested in what was happening in foreign countries because of her missionary union work at church and close friends who were missionaries in Indonesia. She always enjoyed getting to know people in our community from other countries and learning about their culture, especially the foods they cooked and ate. She never denigrated their differences, and even admired them.

Neither my mother nor my father talked openly disparagingly about black people. Mother thought that using the "n-word" was "low class." Before coming to Durham, I had heard what white people like Mother's friend who claimed not to be prejudiced said about black people: "It's not that I don't like Negroes, it's just that I don't see why we have to go swimming with them." In Durham, I also knew people such as our next-door neighbor, who hired a black housekeeper and babysitter. She treated this woman as one of her family at home but made racist comments in all-white company.

These kinds of overt racist conversations, however, were the exceptions in how I learned prejudicial attitudes toward black people when I was growing up. People around me communicated their biases in much more indirect ways. Stereotyping of people by race or religion was transmitted when white adults, my parents included, asked about or noted a person's race (or religion) as a way of explaining a situation or the way people acted. It was usually subtle—noting certain people's knowledge or talents (or lack of them) and a mention in that same breath of their race or nationality. Sometimes the evaluation was so subtle as to be non-verbal. A raised eyebrow, a sigh, pursed lips. Thus, I learned in an unconscious way that my parents or other adults in my life believed that black people were different from white people in ways that may have contributed to their poverty and lack of education. In this way, I learned that black people were less ambitious, slower, more concerned with status symbols than savings, more willing to be on welfare. And there was no counterbalancing or concomitant critique of the systemic causes of racial disparities. Nobody I was around was calling out racism as a factor in any of the problems black people were facing.

Thus, the way I learned about race was not so much in long discussions of white superiority or through racial slurs but in small conversations in which race was noticed and associated with difference and also with judgment about that difference. I resisted even this subtle racism when I could see it, but I didn't always see it. I wanted to be and thought that I was immune to racial prejudice, but I was embedded in my white world, and that meant that the bias I learned, even if unconsciously, was part of me because it was a part of that world.

While I had my personal adolescent identity storm brewing, I was also aware of a tearing of the larger social fabric. Being close to two universities, I saw evidence of upheaval—resistance to the Vietnam War, women's liberation, concern about the environment, teenage runaways (some from my church), drugs and overall disillusion with the status quo. Opposition to the war in Vietnam, unthinkable initially, grew with the nightly viewing of the deaths and suffering of American GIs and Vietnamese civilians. We began to question why we were there.

I was in the middle of a mix of shifting women's and men's roles, faster communication via mass media, the use of mind-altering drugs, and the introduction of Eastern philosophies into popular culture. The birth control pill, loss of faith in our government, veterans coming back traumatized from a war that made no sense to them, concern about a degrading environment and increased secularism were transforming the American "Leave It to Beaver," "Father Knows Best" family and ideals. Once the Pandora's box that allowed us to question authority opened up, everything flew out at once. In the midst of this social change was the civil rights movement, and ending school segregation was a critical component of the fight to end racial inequalities.

* * *

Until the assassination of Dr. Martin Luther King Jr. when I was in the seventh grade, I was only vaguely aware of the racial tensions present in Durham. On that night in April 1968, I was in the living room watching *The Mod Squad* when a news bulletin reported that Dr. King had been fatally shot. I knew who Dr. King was; I had seen him on television and knew he was a civil rights activist, though I did not know a lot more about him. When I heard of his assassination, I was sad in a general way about the loss of someone trying to do something good and horrified at the violence. I also felt the worry of my parents that there would be more violence because of this murder. There was rioting in town, and fires. We had curfews and a day off from school. Students talked about the curfew, but our teachers did not discuss the assassination in our classes; they were all too nervous. Most of what I knew I saw on television and in the newspapers. Just a couple of months later, I woke to news of the assassination of Bobby Kennedy, and that summer I saw images in newspapers and on television of cities across the country torn apart and blazing. But all that seemed far away and unrelated to my life.

Everything that was swirling around me at 15—school, family, church, faith, and what was going on in the bigger world—influenced how I felt about my assignment to Hillside and my engagement with what I found there. I brought all of this with me as I became part of the social experiment of school desegregation at Hillside High School during the fall semester of 1970.

Cindy Waszak (third row from bottom; sixth from left) at
Rogers-Herr Junior High pep rally.
Photo courtesy Rogers-Herr Yearbook, 1967-68

FIVE

Going to Whitted
With the White Kids

LaHoma

My resentment toward Whitted Junior High School ripened and matured as the first day of school neared. I was giving up so much: my friends, my teachers, my beautiful new school. For what? I loathed the idea of going to Whitted—it was old, it was run-down, it was on the other side of town, and I just didn't want to go there. It was not in my neighborhood.

Shepard's new brick façade and the surrounding vicinity were much more appealing; new homes lined the sidewalk to the school, and I had grown accustomed to walking the mile and a half back home with my friends. Most of my frustration with the new school assignment to Whitted revolved around having to walk a different route to school. Even though the walk was exactly the same distance, just thinking about the walk from Whitted was emotionally and psychologically more stress inducing, making it seem longer. Facing the change to my day-to-day routine just didn't seem fair, especially when I felt that I wasn't getting anything worth having in return for the disruption. For me, going to school was about more than just attending classes at any particular school. The ritual of getting to and from school took on great importance, and I bemoaned this distressing change in how I got to and from school. Once a week, for example, on my way home from Shepard, I would stop for piano lessons. My piano teacher, Mrs. Reeves, lived on the corner of Lawson and Sima, conveniently on my route from school. Mrs. Reeves had a small piano studio in her home for young black students. I never became much of a piano player despite the eight years of piano lessons, but the proximity of her studio to my home and its location along my path from school guaranteed that I was a decent player and rarely missed my weekly lessons. The lessons inspired my love and appreciation for music. I learned the notes; I could read music and make beautiful chords. And if I practiced, I could get through most of my assigned pieces. Mrs. Reeves held yearly recitals, and we were required to learn two or three pieces to play "by heart."

Annually, we were evaluated by the North Carolina Piano Guild to assess our level of accomplishment in classical pieces. I developed advanced proficiencies with several Bach and Beethoven selections, to the delight of Mrs. Reeves, who looked forward to showcasing her troupe of budding black piano performers before the wider community of family and friends. Once I changed schools, going to her studio became increasingly burdensome, and within weeks of beginning at Whitted, I quit my piano lessons.

When students started complaining that the new assignments required longer and more challenging commuting distances to school, we were introduced to the word "busing," although it technically did not involve getting on a school bus. Instead we were given vouchers to ride the Durham city buses. I didn't start taking the bus right away, but eventually I succumbed to the urging of my peers. A bus stopped right outside my house.

My friends from the adjoining streets, Joyce and Phyllis, had already started taking the bus. There was another stop at the top of the hill, and they would catch the bus when it stopped at the bottom of the hill—directly in front of my house. I hated taking the bus because most of the good seats were occupied when I boarded. I would have to stand until we reached downtown, where we changed buses.

This transportation arrangement worked out until I started to participate in extracurricular activities. On those afternoons, I could not make it to the bus to get downtown to make the transfer in front of Woolworth's. I would have to walk the mile and a half home by myself. I could control when and where I walked, past houses that became more and more familiar, waving to people sitting on their porches. I could also stop at the "mom and pop" places on the corner of Alston or Ridgeway Avenue, just before I reached home, which I liked to do when I had a few pennies for a treat.

I also hated taking the bus because it seemed that it took forever to get to school, and I had to get up extra early to catch it. We also had to ask for a transfer ticket so we wouldn't have to pay for taking a second bus to school. If you forgot to ask for the transfer or lost it before getting on the next bus, you had to pay full price.

Despite these challenges, I often took the bus because of bad weather or just to go downtown with my friends. Downtown was a great place to see lots of other junior high and high school kids. Somewhere in the sea of black faces there may have been a few white students making the same trek across town, but they were invisible to me. Downtown was also where we met boys—boys from other schools, but more important, from other parts of town.

Learning about boys was a preoccupation, but I also needed to learn a few things about teenage girls. We often did stupid things and instigated fights over silly matters—territory, pride, possessions, boyfriends, girlfriends, and anything else we could think to fight about. Pulling hair and throwing punches were the norm, although sometimes a knife would be pulled out to stress the seriousness of the offense and bring greater attention to a particular grievance.

I was once drawn into a fight to defend my honor because the girl had said something I didn't like.

"Don't call me names," I said, clenching my fists.

But after this bigger and much badder girl pulled out a knife, I got smart and ran away as fast as I could. I was so scared that I promised God that I would never allow myself to be drawn into a meaningless fight again. I learned a valuable life lesson, and since that day I have seen myself as a peacemaker, conflict resolver, and avoider of all physical displays of aggression or violence—especially with people bigger than I.

* * *

The first few days and weeks at Whitted proved not as bad as I had imagined. As the months rolled by, my outgoing personality and desire to please the teachers surpassed my anxieties. I was in the modern dance group, cheerleading, honor society, student council and the band. I made new friends, and I relished my expanding circle of influence at school, even though I still longed for dear old Shepard. And then there were the school athletic competitions, which forced us to claim bragging rights of superiority for our school.

Durham City Schools' efforts to integrate Whitted were most evident in the membership of student activities and organizations. The 1971 Honor Society at Whitted included its first white students. We were friends because we had mutual academic interests and goals, but we rarely interacted with each other outside school. We were all nice to each other, but Honor Society meetings were where our lives together began and ended. We certainly did not hang out or spend time together after school. Most of these students came from the Forest Hills and Duke University area and were children of privilege and prominent political figures in Durham. Despite the change in Durham school board policies, that they came to Whitted was surprising and that they remained—perplexing. I overheard black adult conversations suggesting that it would just be a matter of time before these white students would transfer to private schools, since many others had already made the decision to leave the public school system.

* * *

Much has been written about the black students forced to endure all-white schools, but very little about those white students who elected to remain in an all-black school setting when, often, their social and economic status provided them with other options. Most of the white students who remained at Whitted during those first couple of years continued on to Hillside to complete high school. I was not aware of their struggles, did not ask about their problems and lacked curiosity about their daily lives. They were, again, largely invisible to me.

I was caught up in the busyness of my own existence, and I did not feel any particular need to reach out to them. We were all the victims of our Southern traditions and had low expectations for anything beyond a friendly "hey" to the sprinkling of white students here and there. Besides, they seemed fine. Later I would discover that although this was certainly true in some cases, there were definitely exceptions. For the life of me, I couldn't tell you who those struggling white students were.

* * *

I loved going to school, reading books, and doing homework, and I generally excelled in my classes. I was rewarded for good penmanship, studiousness, and responsiveness to authority. I increasingly took on more activities, eventually leading to my election as the student body president in ninth grade.

I still can't explain exactly how I won that election, because it still felt as though we were the "new" kids—the interlopers. My friends and I were outsiders to the Fayetteville Street and Enterprise neighborhood surrounding Whitted, and we were definitely the geographical minority in the school. I was not particularly well known, and I was not liked by the majority of students because of the other names I had acquired, including "teacher's pet" and "stuck up." So even though I ran for student body president at the urging of one of my teachers, I did not think I stood a chance against my more popular opponents.

I was elated when I won, but I thought that if I was puzzled over the outcome, I couldn't imagine how some of the other students were feeling. But no one challenged the results, so

I spent the ninth grade learning how to carefully walk the tightropes among administration, teachers and my peers, both black and white. The white students were easy—they did not aspire to traditional leadership positions in the school, although they were often the top academic performers. My fellow black students presented an array of amusing and annoying challenges, mostly teases and teacher's-pet name-calling, which I could mostly ignore. But this short tenure with student government was sufficiently difficult that it kept me from seeking similar positions in high school.

With time, I realized that the student government president position was largely titular and ceremonial and carried little sway with the majority of students. I was an ally of the teachers and administrators, who were probably relieved that I did not appear to be someone who would disturb the budding racial integration efforts. The last thing the people working at the school needed during those early days of integration was someone to challenge authority.

I spent a lot of time with the teachers and administrators. I loved most of them, especially Ms. Mamie Perry, who was in charge of the Honor Society, and Ms. Edith Johnson, the physical education and dance group teacher. I rationalized that, even though junior high had not turned out the way I planned, I still had great teachers and adults who were focused on my success. They were also the disciplinarians who ran Whitted with steely wills and wooden rulers. Mostly the rulers were used to single out the person or object of their anger or displeasure. But sometimes it served other purposes. We were more terrified of these two women because of the threat of their disapproval than anything else. Nobody wanted to get on these teachers' bad sides.

I think I understand now why they were so loved and feared. They challenged us to excel by demonstrating how much they cared for us, how much they wanted us to succeed. They expected us to do well. Their role is one of the reasons that some teachers from that era think that integration was the worst thing to happen to black children in Durham. The black teachers held positions of prestige and power in the community, and parents held them in great esteem. Black parents were also accountable to these teachers in a way, because they would see them outside of school, in the grocery stores or churches. When I described this book project to my godmother, Mrs. Smith, she lamented that the power dynamic between teachers and students changed, diminishing as integration meant that parents and teachers no longer came from the same communities or represented the same interests.

* * *

Mrs. Smith, now 99 years old, reflected on that period of her professional life:

"I was one of the first black teachers at Rogers-Herr, arriving in 1970, and I stayed four years. I didn't like it because the teachers were so prejudiced, and they decided that the students from the projects (Cornwallis) didn't know anything so they didn't need to teach them anything. Mr. Schooler (who was the principal at Shepard at the time) picked the teachers who would go to Rogers-Herr as part of the integration effort, and I was picked.

"When I got there, I found out that they had resources that we did not have at Shepard—books, a nice library, IQ tests, instruments, and other resources. I was surprised to see that these resources were only available to the white students.

"Integration benefited some of the students; in fact, there were some people who wanted their kids to be there. In Durham, there was quiet resistance to desegregation, but there was a lot of resentment about the whole situation.

"Black people brought a lot of money into Durham through the various institutions like North Carolina Mutual Life Insurance Company, the largest black-owned business in the world, and they were able to negotiate favorable circumstances for some black students in Durham.

"But there were parts of Durham that were exclusively white, like Forest Hills and Hope Valley, and where black people better not go. Black police could only arrest black people. These were the communities closest to Rogers-Herr and Hillside.

"In my opinion, integration was good for the students who could take advantage of it. The 'project' kids seemed to resent being there, and their parents wouldn't let the white teachers touch them, so the teachers stopped trying to discipline them. Of course this was not the way we were used to dealing with black children in our black schools. The discipline issues were different, and they continued to deteriorate after integration. There were also differences in how the students were treated, and the expectations and consequently discipline of black students were low.

"Black parents from the working class and low socioeconomic circumstances might not come to meetings because of their fear of being judged by white teachers. I always suspected that kids know when you like them, and there was a feeling that the white teachers didn't like the black ones anyway, so they just left them to fail."

* * *

Daily school life at Whitted had been greatly affected by our teachers. They were tough, tough, tough but fair. If you displeased them or did something to offend their sensibilities, you knew it IMMEDIATELY. We were expected to carry ourselves as young ladies and gentlemen and to represent the school and our families.

Our teachers would send home students who they believed had not paid sufficient attention to personal hygiene after gym class. They taught us pride in our appearance and the need to respect one's self by wearing dresses and skirts of the appropriate length. These attitudes ran counter to the prevailing fashion trends of the day, the miniskirt era, but our teachers had no qualms about sending us home to change clothes when we were deemed to have violated the dress code. I came as close as I could to the "decent v. danger" lines that we imagined our teachers had, but luckily for me I escaped the judgment and punishment that I saw befall fellow classmates. It was usually hard to get anything past my mother, anyway.

Ms. Perry was most focused on academic achievement and attentiveness to scholarship. As the social studies and English teacher, she was a stickler for grammar, penmanship, diction, and vocabulary. I once made the mistake of telling a peer to keep his "damn hands off me." Unfortunately, Ms. Perry was within earshot. She reprimanded me in front of the class for such a vulgar display of language, and then kept me after school to write 100 times on the board: "I will not use curse words, I will not use curse words." The remnants of this punishment linger to the present time because I still have a strong aversion to cursing. Who says eighth-grade teachers don't have power over your life?

I tried to stay on the good side of Ms. Perry, and she rewarded my efforts with high praise. But she was not one to be crossed. If I thought I was one of her favorites because of my high grades in her classes, she was quick to remind me that I was just another student to her—a student who needed to be taught to respect the rules.

Take bathroom breaks, for example. We were allowed to go to the bathroom only during class breaks. Because of the large number of female students compared to the size of the bathroom, Ms. Perry would allow only one group of girls to go at a time. To prevent loitering and shenanigans, she timed us. One day, the group of girls to which I had been assigned took what Ms. Perry must have considered too much time. She was waiting for us when we returned. She lined all the offending students up against the wall, and we were each spanked with the wooden rulers—for failing to return in a timely fashion and failing to consider the needs of our fellow classmates, who had to wait the few extra minutes it had taken us to return to class. I was embarrassed and humiliated. Although I had seen her inflict her wrath on others, I had always been spared.

I heard other students snickering, "Even LaHoma got spanked."

That day I learned another lifelong lesson—that students will respect you if they believe that the discipline is fairly distributed. My dear Ms. Perry ran a tight but fair ship, though I always wondered what would have happened if there had been white students with us because I never saw white students being disciplined that way.

Ms. Johnson oversaw the modern dance group that included only girls who would respect her rules for conduct. None of the white students joined the dance group, either from lack of interest or lack of confidence—I cannot say. Ms. Johnson did not select girls based on dance talent, experience or body type. Her philosophy was that if you really wanted to dance and demonstrated willingness to practice and learn the routines, she would be willing to accept you into the group.

Ms. Johnson started each year with a large group of willing souls who thought they could keep up with the rules and be allowed to perform at school programs, pageants and the annual dance performance. Sounds simple enough, but the annual dance performance always had fewer girls than had started at the first practice. Ms. Johnson's strict conduct policies proved more effective in selecting her dancers than any other screening process.

Ms. Johnson also used the dance group as a recruiting pool for the cheerleading squad. She was not as democratic or inclusive with this group. Tryouts were held for the junior varsity and varsity teams, and you needed to demonstrate general athletic abilities, including flexibility and coordination.

When I entered Whitted, I never thought of myself as a cheerleader. Besides, I couldn't do the splits, cartwheels and somersaults that I thought were necessary. But I learned I liked performing in front of crowds, and with just a teeny bit of encouragement from my friends—and sizing up the competition—I decided, why not?

So I begged my mom to sign me up for a few private gymnastics classes before the tryouts. I thought I could learn everything I needed to know in a couple of lessons. The white instructor promised to help me learn how to do all the impressive feats that would turn me into the next Cathy Rigby. I didn't care about any of that, especially because I had never seen black gymnasts on any local or national teams. I just wanted to learn to jump high, turn a cartwheel with confidence and gain sufficient flexibility to muster up a decent split so I could make the squad.

I practiced with diligence for a few weeks to give myself a chance of making the final cut, or at the least, avoid embarrassing myself in front of my peers. I could not think of anything worse than that; I thought I could be forgiven for not measuring up to the high standards of Ms. Johnson, but looking stupid in front of my peers would be the worst possible outcome. I also worked on a dance routine—one of the three try-out requirements, along with a chant and yell (with enthusiasm of course) and some sort of stunt (cartwheel, flip, somersault, split, etc.).

The day of tryouts arrived. My mom had pressed my hair the night before so it glistened. My clothes were clean and tidy, my shorts were short (but not too short), and I had on the double-down socks popular in the day. I sat patiently with at least 50 other hopeful candidates. We all watched and applauded for each girl's routine—regardless of how good it was. It was us against Ms. Johnson.

Finally it was my turn: "LaHoma Smith," I heard Ms. Johnson say. I took my position and began my chant to the tune of the hit show, "The Adams Family":

Dadadadum (Clap clap) Da dadadum (Clap clap)

Da dadadumDa dadadum

Da dada...dum....(Kick ball chain step...Clap clap)

We're rough and we're tough...We really got the stuff... You can't mess with us...

The Viking family...(Moving my hips and shuffling my feet from side to side)

Da...da da dum (Clap clap)......Da dadadum(Clap clap)......Da dadadum....Da dada dum....

Da dada…dum….(Clap clap)

Pose….Smile…..High spread eagle jump…..Pose again…..
High kick… Cheer with pump fist ….

Go Vikings!!!

Then I ran really fast, spread my legs and turned upside
down into a cartwheel…

(Nailed it!)

"Go Vikings!!!!" I exclaimed one more time for good
measure.

There was polite applause from the other girls waiting their
turns. I took my seat on the bleachers. I could not read Ms.
Johnson's face. She was probably a good poker player, because
nothing about her expression betrayed her thoughts about each
performance. You had no idea if you had done a good or lousy
job by her standards. Did I kick high enough? Did I yell loud
enough? Were my legs straight enough in my cartwheel? Did I
move my hips enough? Or maybe I moved them too much, and
Ms. Johnson would think that I was too "grown" to be a good
representative for the school? No way to know.

We waited for the remaining girls to try their luck, and then
it was over. Ms. Johnson thanked everyone for coming out,
reminded us that only eight to 10 girls would be chosen, and
that the lucky few would see their names posted outside the
gym. She said that everyone was a winner, or something to that
effect, but by then, we were all filing out, relieved that was over
while calculating our prospects, given what we had seen from
the competition.

One week went by. Then two—an eternity. Finally, without
ceremony, Ms. Johnson posted the list of girls who had made
the squad on the door outside the gym. I hastily scrolled down
the alphabetical list of names on the Junior Varsity list …

Parker, Reynolds, Sims, Stevens ... there was no Smith. I backed away to reflect on the realization of this defeat. I knew I was not the best, but I thought that I had done at least as good or better than any of the girls whose names appeared on the list.

As I turned to go, I heard another girl saying,

"LaHoma you made it." Annoyed with such cruel teasing, I turned to see who was mocking me.

"No, I didn't," I said, and turned away from that terrible door with the terrible list. Someone else pushed me back in the direction of the door. This time I noticed another list. My friend pointed to my name.

"See ... on the Varsity squad."

I looked—terrified that she was wrong—and then terrified that she was right. There it was: "LaHoma Smith." I hadn't even considered looking at the names for the Varsity squad—the current members on that squad were all ninth graders. But there it was, in black and white.

I was excited, then scared. I had never been a cheerleader before, and now I was on the varsity squad for Whitted!

Go Vikings!

For the remainder of my time at Whitted, I was a varsity cheerleader. We traveled to all the local junior high schools to cheer our sports teams. The visit to Rogers-Herr made a lasting impression. This was the school that Cindy had attended. What nice facilities they had—even nicer than my beloved Shepard! The bathrooms were light and spacious. The building and equipment all seemed new. We played the game, but the outcome seemed to lose its importance as I looked around the building and noticed how much nicer the gym at Rogers-Herr was compared to our old, worn-out bleachers at Whitted. Their uniforms seemed much nicer and newer than ours. Even though integration had occurred, their varsity cheerleaders were all white, just as our varsity cheerleaders were all black. But I didn't care. I loved my school.

* * *

Most of our teachers were women, but there was definitely male influence at Whitted. Besides our principal, Mr. McAllister, the main male role model for me was Mr. Hodge, the band director. I did not play a band instrument when I started at Whitted, but I had taken piano lessons for eight years and loved music, knew my notes and could carry a tune. Mr. Hodge encouraged students who were interested in music to try out for the band, and then he would assign you an instrument to learn.

I knew I couldn't play the piano in the band, so I yearned to play the clarinet or flute because those were the instruments usually assigned to the girls. To my horror, Mr. Hodge assigned me to play the French horn, an odd-shaped gigantic piece of heavy equipment that I noticed was typically played only by the guys. I had never even heard of the French horn until Mr. Hodge assigned it to me.

When I protested, he smiled, gave me a knowing pat on the head, and told me I would be fine. I always wondered why Mr. Hodge assigned me the French horn—maybe because even at that age, I was one of the taller girls and he had enough petite ones playing the flutes and clarinets. I looked over and saw that one of my equally sturdy friends had been assigned to play the saxophone.

One of the worst things about playing the French horn was the bulky, awkward shape of the case, which made carrying it difficult. But I learned to play the instrument. I was one of four

French horn players, and the only girl. I took a bad situation and made it worse by developing a crush on one of the older, male French horn players. This made being in the band more fun, but playing in the French horn section itself was daunting. We were often the subject of whispers and jeers—especially when Mr. Hodge would call on the French horn section for attention or to practice a refrain that we had brutalized.

By ninth grade, I had earned first chair even though I was only a fair French horn player at best. Mr. Hodge's passion and ability to inspire his young musicians, regardless of talent or possession of an instrument, helped advance the musical fortunes of many Whitted students that year. They were then ready to join the dynamic marching band of Hillside High School.

* * *

Every once in a while, my neighborhood friends and I would avoid going directly home from school. We would linger near Five Points—close to the intersection of West Main and East Chapel Hill streets in downtown Durham—waiting for and eventually catching the bus transfer that would take us home. We strolled down the sidewalk, looking in the windows, avoiding the stores where we knew teenage black girls would not be welcome. The sit-ins of the 1960s were now more than 10 years past, and while we were able to order food at the Woolworth's without a problem, unspoken rules about how to comport oneself in this evolving climate prevailed. I did not fully understand what it all meant, but I knew better than to question, and even more important, I knew how to conduct myself. Besides, there were lots of places to shop downtown. Belk-Leggett, one of the most popular department stores, featured a beautiful display window the length of the store. The styles and prices were well beyond my eighth-grade budget, but that could not stop me from looking.

* * *

Black people had started shopping downtown. The civil rights movement and the call to dismantle segregation by boycotting businesses had done much to make shopping in most places possible, but it didn't mean that it was always comfortable. Other stores on Main Street were Montaldo's, Thalhimers, Montgomery Ward and Baldwins. Black people initially entered these places cautiously to see how white people would react. Older residents stayed alert, and most expected someone to ask them to leave. But there were no major incidents as Durham came to symbolize a progressive model of successful race relations—at least in the retail sector.

I could think of no excuse to enter any of those stores anyway, because my mother made most of my clothes—a point of constant conflict between her and me. Why did she have to make ALL my Sunday dresses? Why couldn't we get one of these store-bought dresses once in a while? My closest friends knew my agony and teased me mercilessly. I begged Mama so much and made such a fuss that by the time I got to high school, she relented and allowed me to purchase an Easter outfit from Baldwins for church. I can't get into that dress now, but I still own it.

When I was hanging out with my friends in junior high school, we didn't talk about race a lot, but we understood our boundaries. We knew about Dr. Martin Luther King Jr., knew about the marches and the riots, heard the "I Have a Dream" speech, but knew, deep down in our souls, that we hadn't quite arrived, even though we were now going to school with white kids. We also were supposed to be able to go anywhere in town, but our preferred stores were the ones where we knew we would be tolerated and could afford to buy something. Only a handful of stores fit those criteria: Kress Department Store, Raylass, and Rose's. We could buy candy, books, magazines, records, socks and underwear, or toiletries. The all-white staff of clerks and shopping attendants pretended to ignore us until we were ready to pay for something. But we felt their suspicious eyes following us around the store to make sure we did not mess up anything or leave with unpaid merchandise. Their stares never bothered my friends and me because our intention was not to steal, and we never let them spoil the fun we had looking at the beautiful wares.

One day shortly before Christmas as we waited for the bus, a few of my girlfriends and I did our usual walk through Raylass to admire all the things we planned to tell our parents we wanted for Christmas or that we hoped might be presents we'd give each other. Joyce saw it first and let out a scream.

"Look at this, look at this!" she implored.

We all ran to where she was standing, as she held up something that I had never before seen—a black baby doll. We circled to examine its features.

"Look," Joyce said, "she's the same color we are."

I marveled at her hair, her outfit, her makeup, and the smile on her face. But mostly we just stared, because in all of our 14 years, this was the first time we had ever seen a doll with our skin color. I didn't know how I felt about it.

All the dolls that I had ever seen in Durham were white. Where did this doll come from? Who made it? Joyce exclaimed that she had to have it, and the other girls soon joined in her enthusiasm. Yes, we would tell our mothers, our aunts, our grandmothers, about our find. The only problem was that because we were all now teenagers who had outgrown dolls, the request might seem a bit ridiculous. And purchasing a doll for myself when I was also purchasing tampons and sanitary pads seemed incongruous.

Joyce was unfazed. She proclaimed the doll as THE item to own to her sister, Phyllis, and our circle of friends, Barbara and LaVerne. Because our parents would probably think it was crazy to buy dolls for their teenage daughters, we fixated on another group of possible financiers—the boys we were "talking to" or "dating." (I use the term "dating" loosely, since none of us could actually go out of the house on an actual date.) Rather, these were boys we talked to over the phone, or flirted with and stole kisses from whenever we had the opportunity.

Joyce insisted that the guy she was dating would buy her a black baby doll for Christmas. Others followed suit, and soon we were probably the largest collection of unofficial advertisers for the Raylass black baby doll collection. We should have earned commissions for all the sales we generated.

I personally never caught the black baby doll frenzy, though. I didn't have a steady boyfriend then, and even if I had, I am sure that I would have wanted something more appropriate for my age, like a watch. As companies started to understand the sales potential of the non-white doll market, and more and more brown dolls came on the scene, we began to see more ethnically diverse dolls. But I never bothered to replace the white dolls that littered my room, and I had largely forgotten this episode. It wasn't until I graduated from college that companies really started to mass-produce black dolls. Some 40 years later, on one of my overseas assignments, my teenage daughter and I were shopping in an upscale department store in Cameroon in central west African when she wandered away from me and returned a few minutes later.

"Mom," she asked, "why are there no black dolls for sale here?"

* * *

As baby dolls faded from my purview, they were replaced with other preoccupations more fitting to teenage girls—teenage boys and avoiding pregnancy. Although Roe v. Wade would become the law of the land in the year after my departure from Whitted, pregnancy and what to do if you ever got pregnant were hot topics among junior high girls, both black and white. I had already adopted a fail-proof method for preventing an unwanted pregnancy. In fact, my mother should have marketed her own brand of contraception, because she prevented me from experimenting with any type of risky sexual behavior in my formative years despite my curiosity and the dares and double dares of my friends. The fear of my mother's wrath kept my legs tightly shut together.

I was jealous of the girls who had begun dating, whose parents allowed them to leave the house in the company of boys, or even permitted them to have extended visiting hours. My parents—no, correction—my mother was having none of that. She never missed an opportunity to explain to me what the consequences would be if I: (a) had sex before marriage (b) got pregnant, and (c) had a baby before I got married. Whenever I was evenly slightly tempted to deviate from her warnings, the thought of my mama throwing me into the streets, with no clothes, no food, and no way to take care of myself, kept me virtuous long after I had the urge to be otherwise. Now I know that she never would have followed through on those threats, but I managed to test her unconditional love for me in other ways.

There were the occasional whispers about girls who got pregnant and suffered terrible consequences—beaten by their parents, shipped off to live with relatives out of state or subjected to some other unimaginable fate. One especially traumatic rumor for us was a young girl in my class who had tried to self-abort using a coat hanger. This gossip was passed from girl to girl to remind us of the shame and of the deadly consequences of sexual activity. These warnings had no effect on some of my classmates, who, according to gossip, continued to experiment in dangerous ways, but they scared the bejeezus out of me.

That's not to say I didn't flirt, have boyfriends, lots of boyfriends, and even make out under the right circumstances. It's just that nothing convinced me that the promise of pleasure would outweigh my mother's promise of pain and suffering. It also helped that none of the boys I liked in junior high school seemed that interested in sex either. THAT STUFF, I told myself, could wait until I was older.

Illegal drug use was not common in my circle of friends, but we were becoming increasingly interested in alcohol. From the hit TV series *The Mod Squad* we heard of white kids using all kinds of crazy stuff, but I was never exposed to anything like that—just the legal liquid. I would take a sniff here, a sip there. Boone's Farm 99 was the cheapest stuff we could get our hands on. It smelled disgusting and tasted yucky. Sometimes I gave in to peer pressure, but I never fully appreciated the appeal of drinking until you couldn't walk straight. I was too wrapped up in my activities to get sidetracked with that stuff. Even cigarettes were of no interest to me, but we knew people our age who were already pack-a-day smokers.

But back to the boys.

It is odd, but I was never really attracted to the boys from church or even the ones from Whitted, aside from the French horn player. Yes, I flirted with them, but no one lingered on my mind once the moment (or hour) of contact was over. No, the guys I longed for were the ones who had dropped out of school (or were close to dropping out of school), whom I met on our block's corner, or at house parties or downtown when we waited for our buses. The boys who got our attention were older, lived in distant neighborhoods unbeknownst to our parents, and therefore possessed a dangerous and mysterious allure. They were always a little older than we were, attending one of the high schools in Durham, or not, which added another layer of risky excitement.

Part of the fun of these relationships was simply trying to arrange to meet the guys. Because none of my friends were old enough to drive, we spent countless hours whispering and talking about how we were going to get a call or note out to the boy of interest to meet somewhere we had no business being.

The success of these encounters also required that the whole event be experienced en masse. Translation: We always group dated. In those days, it was the only way to spend time with a special person. These days, I think about it as the only way, whether we realized it or not, to ensure safety and protection from guys we didn't know that well, who got too friendly, or who wanted the relationship to progress too quickly. If three was a crowd, then imagine how impossible it was to do anything with at least eight other people around.

My friends and I delighted in discussing and plotting our next group rendezvous with our latest boyfriends. We would hang around the bus stop to see the North Durham boys in town on Wednesday, then meet the Fayetteville Street boys at a house party on Friday night, and then the Four Oaks boys would pick us up on the corner on Saturday night to drive around town. We would get dropped off two to three hours later, on the same block, and then we walked home, our parents never the wiser.

This foolhardy activity continued throughout my junior high school years. We were especially active in the summer months, when we had more time, and could bring even more groups of guys into the dating mix. Only one rule existed for expanding our network—there had to be a guy for each of us, so, in principle, we could not date a guy who didn't have at least four other friends he could introduce us to. It really didn't matter if you liked the guy you met, as long as he was available when the rest of the crew showed up so you would at least be assured of having someone to talk to.

We talked about and compared the guys to our favorite male musicians: the Jackson Five, Marvin Gaye, and Smokey Robinson. Who looked the most like Michael? Like Jermaine (my favorite)? After each encounter, we discussed every detail, critiquing every aspect, from the clothes they wore to the words they uttered. "What's wrong with his teeth?" my junior high friend Karen complained about her latest recruit. "He really knows how to take care of his 'fro," Janet observed. We also rated them against other love (or like) interests. We assured one another with hardly a shred of evidence that the chosen guy (of the hour) really liked her.

One beautiful Saturday evening, we arranged to meet the Four Oaks boys. My friends and I congregated early on the block as usual, lying to our parents that we would be spending the evening at Ann's house. We waited for the boys, searching out every car that passed, because we had no idea who would be driving or what type of vehicle it would be. Finally, the oldest of the Four Oaks crew, Steve, a senior at Hillside, pulled up in his daddy's Pontiac. One of the other guys showed up a minute later in another car, so the five of us (girls) piled into one of the two cars—three in the first car, two in the second. We circled the neighborhood a few times, one car following closely behind the other, looking for a quiet place to pull over and talk. Then Sharon starting laughing and shouting out of the window to oncoming cars:

"Help ... we're being kidnapped!" she hollered.

"She's crazy!" Steve shouted to the other car. But it was hilarious so we laughed, which egged Sharon on to continue her proclamations:

"Help me! Help me!" she yelled. The tape decks were blasting, and we were all singing and laughing.

The lead car turned onto a side street, headed down an alleyway, and slowed. The second car followed suit. Headlights dimmed as both cars came to a stop. Everybody got out of the cars in silence as we looked around to make sure we were alone. Then someone said something, and another chimed in. Another person giggled, and then one of the boys brought out something to drink. And the party was on, the volume from the tape deck turned up again, and the dancing, singing and laughing continued. A couple slipped away a few hundred feet, presumably to hug and kiss. The rest of us ignored them. We turned up the volume of the music.

Suddenly a bright light flashed toward us. I adjusted my eyes to focus on who it was. Everyone ran back to the cars. A voice barked, amplified by a megaphone:

"Police. Don't move. Stay where you are."

A black officer got out of his car. A white officer also got out but stayed behind. The black officer approached our cars, slowly, peering inside one, then the other. This took forever, as I kept thinking one thing: "My parents are going to kill me." Finally, he spoke:

"What are you kids doing out here?"

We all looked at one another, and someone (not me) said something stupid like, "Talking." The officer gave us a disgusted look, and countered, "We didn't notice a lot of talking when we drove up." He then asked the most sobering question: "Do your parents know you are here?"

The very thought that he would let them know sickened me. I stood stone silent, contemplating the punishment that awaited me.

"Yes, they do," Sharon lied, knowing that her parents would kill her if they knew where she was. I didn't say a word.

"How old are you?" the officer asked.

"Sixteen," Sharon lied again. I had to give her credit—she was quick on her feet.

"Who was screaming out of the cars?" the black police officer asked. "Is someone here in trouble?"

All our eyes turned toward Sharon again. She had been the one shouting from the car earlier, not out of fright, but with delight. Now, we were going to jail because she could not keep her mouth shut and for lying to the police. Her big sister explained that Sharon wasn't screaming, she was singing a song.

We rolled our eyes in collective disgust as one lie trickled out after another.

The black officer went back to the patrol car to confer with his white counterpart. I considered my fate and wondered if I would ever see daylight again once my parents found out. Another few minutes passed, and the officer walked back to us.

"OK kids. This is a warning. Go home. You are on private property, and you are underage. I am not going to think about what you are doing, or what you could be doing, but you can't do it here, so go home. If I see you out here again, I am going to take you to jail and call your parents."

We scampered back into the cars before he could change his mind and drove away. The Four Oaks boys dropped us off on the corner. The five of us girls stood outside for a few minutes to regroup, cursing Sharon for her big mouth, and thanking God for allowing us to return home without a police escort.

The charm of group dating was broken.

* * *

Black working class parents have the reputation of being strict adherents to the biblical reference "spare the rod, spoil the child," to paraphrase several verses from Proverbs (Old Testament) and Hebrews (New Testament). The belief was that if you really want your children to behave and do well in life, then you need to discipline them, using force if necessary. The reasoning was that parents should let their children know the boundaries for self-preservation, and if the punishment seemed harsh, it was for their own good. And no parents wanted good for their children more than my parents.

Years later, they shared that they had seen what happened to people who had challenged Jim Crow laws, and they had seen what happened to black kids who did not behave. Thus, they sought to protect us from our selves by physically reminding us by a flash of a belt or twig, whenever we disobeyed, to prevent us from resisting authority, white or black. I noticed that Marcia and Jan, my young "Brady Bunch" TV idols, never experienced this much love from Mike and Carol Brady!

As a girl, I had an additional burden: my mother.

I had a love/hate relationship with my mother from junior high through high school. I adored my father. We were similar in temperament and overall disposition. He rarely raised his voice. He never wandered off course, never solicited answers to unwanted questions. I could persuade my father to trust me to do almost anything as long as it was not immoral or illegal.

But Mom was another creature. She questioned my every move, every decision. She challenged everything I did and everything I said, first with an innocent query—then with deadly commentary.

"Are you going to wear that dress? It's too short." She asked and declared.

"Why is that boy calling you so late—decent people don't call other people's houses past 9 o'clock."

I never got a break. She wore me out. I would have to create a strategic offense in my devious 14-year-old brain to counter her inevitable defense to any of my plans for fun and pleasure. Even my friends knew my mother well. Whenever we were planning some new scheme to venture out of parental view, the question was never about my father. It was always, "What are you going to tell your momma?"

To label my mother simply as the disciplinarian would be to minimize the power dynamics in our household. She ruled with absolute supremacy and indifference to the humiliating circumstances into which she sometimes placed me. She had a sharp tongue and an even sharper insight into the inner workings of a young girl's mind.

One summer evening I tested the limits of what I thought was an unreasonably early curfew. Hours past the designated time, I tried to slither past my father, asleep in the chair in front of the television. My mother, sitting in the dark, turned on the bright light in the kitchen to stop me.

"Where have you been?" she barked.

"With my friends like I told you," I lied.

"Which friends?" she countered.

"You know, Yvonne and Charlene."

"Call them right now and let me talk to them."

"It's too late to call them now; I'll call them in the morning," I said.

"No, we will call them now."

I couldn't think of a retort, so I yawned, claimed that I was sleepy, and kept walking toward my bedroom. Wrong idea. She ran up behind me, grabbed my arm, and turned me around— her eyes piercing through me. She pressed me against the wall.

"Were you with a ... boy?"

"Of course not," I lied again.

"Are you sure you were not with a boy?"

Dare I tell another lie?

"No, I was not with a boy, Mother." As I heard yet another lie come out of my mouth, I wondered whether this boy was worth the punishment that I knew was coming for all these lies. Was he really worth this agony? I returned to the moment, my mother still fuming before her dumbfounded, guilty-as-accused, lying daughter.

"It was just a friend," I heard myself say.

"A friend you had to lie about? Was it a boy or a girl, and where were you?"

I couldn't decide whether she would be more disappointed if I told her the truth or if I didn't say anything. I decided to go with the latter and refused to confirm or deny her accusations. She couldn't make me talk, so I just closed my eyes and awaited my fate.

Frustrated with my refusal to further engage with her, she demanded I go to my room. I fell back from her stare and retreated, glad to be away from her. But now the real agony began, because I didn't know what would happen to me. Dad had awakened during the late-night interrogation, but he remained silently on the sidelines, helpless to intervene.

For the remainder of the weekend, my mother didn't speak to me, did not even look at me. Agony. What could she be thinking? Maybe she would forget about it? Maybe my Dad would convince her to go easy on me. But whom was I fooling? I waited some more.

Finally after what seemed like forever, my mother levied my sentence. And it was a doozy. No telephone or privileges outside school for three months.

THREE MONTHS! How could she?

"That's forever!" I protested. This was the beginning of May... so June, July, August! The whole summer!

"Is it?" she asked, and walked away.

But my mother wasn't done making my life miserable. Over the course of the next couple of weeks, I managed to take my bitter medicine. I told a few friends about my predicament, and they were suitably impressed by the harshness of the sentence. They shared their condolences and teased me about the wonderful things I would probably miss over the summer.

School was still in session, so I managed to have a bit of a social life during the day. But as soon as the bell rang, my prison sentence would begin.

One evening, two weeks down and 12 to go into my punishment, we were at the table having dinner, and the phone rang. My mother picked it up.

"Hello," she said sweetly.

"LaHoma?" the caller asked.

"Oh, I'm sorry, but LaHoma has done something very bad, and she has lost her telephone privileges for three months so, no, you can't talk to her. Please do not call back here this summer. Thank you and have a nice day."

She hung up the telephone, looked over at me and smiled sweetly, completely aware of the humiliation I would experience once the details of that telephone call spread through school. Satisfied that my summer fate would now be broadcast throughout my social circle, she smiled again at me—the first time in more than a month—and walked out of the room.

That summer lasted forever, although I gradually earned more freedom from my mother's watchful eyes. I got a job as a camp counselor at W.D. Hill Recreation Center on Fayetteville Street and worked with other junior high and high school students to supervise the daily activities of the younger kids in the community. We walked everywhere, including our weekly excursions to the pool at Hillside Park. Although the public schools were integrated, the swimming pools in Durham largely operated along racial lines. Hillside Park serviced Durham's black community; Meadow Park was for white people only. If integration was so important, I pondered, why didn't they integrate the pools, since the one at Hillside was frequently jammed pack with black kids from all over town. But I didn't lose any sleep over that fact. We had survived the integration experiment at school. The white students had come, they were nice, we were nice, but they had hardly affected anything about the rest of my life.

It was time to move up to Hillside High School.

LaHoma Smith (back row, fourth from left) in the
National Honor Society at Whitted Junior High School.
Courtesy of Whitted Junior High School, 1970-71

SIX

Being White at Hillside High:
A Different World

Cindy
Sophomore Year (1970-1971)

Hillside High School was in a quiet, middle-class residential area—small brick ranch houses across the street from the school, not so different from where I lived, and not far geographically from where I lived. Yet, I had never been in this neighborhood before the first day of school. This neighborhood was just not part of my white world in Durham.

An element of white parents' concerns about their children going to school in black neighborhoods was about their children's safety, but I never felt unsafe at Hillside. The area was not the part of Durham that white people referred to then as "colored town" (if they were polite)—that part of Southern geography where black people, always assumed to be poor, lived. Nor was it what people might refer to as "the ghetto," with its associations with drugs and violent crime.

But the area around the school was still a part of Durham unfamiliar to my family and me, and thus it became an unspoken rule that I was not to be there in the evenings or on weekends. During the three years I attended Hillside, I never saw much more beyond what I could see from where Mother let us out and picked us up in front of the school every day.

When I found out my school assignment that summer, I thought, naively, "This experience will teach me what it is like to be a racial minority." I know now that even being a white minority in a public institution in America could never provide an experience similar to being black in a white world. The advantages experienced by white people compared to non-white people that presumed higher social status and greater freedom to move and speak without constraint were pervasive in Durham and did not disappear when I stepped into the Hillside school building the first day of school—or ever. Going to school at Hillside, however, did provide another world view.

* * *

The school board had expected a black to white ratio of 58 to 42 at Hillside that first year, but in actuality, it was 69 to 31, with an enrollment of about 1,200 students (7). In my college prep classes the proportion of white students was almost half, so I never felt like a minority in the classroom. Hillside had excellent vocational education in subjects such as tailoring, automotive mechanics, and secretarial skills—classes taken by the majority of students, but not me and not my friends.

Teachers also were assigned to schools to reflect the racial composition of the system as a whole. I had memorable teachers—both black and white—during my sophomore year. I know that, in spite of my earlier worries about academic competitiveness, my educational experience was equal to what I would have gotten at Durham High School, and enriched, in a "real world" kind of way, by being at this predominantly black school.

My English teacher my freshman year was a petite white woman, with short, straight brown hair, possibly mid-30s (old to me at the time), who spoke quietly and dressed modestly. She taught me most of what I learned in high school about black writers from the Harlem Renaissance and since. Because it was a required class for everyone, the majority of the class was black.

She challenged us to think differently. She had been teaching at Hillside High School for several years even before desegregation—possibly the only white teacher who had—and was part of that community before the desegregation order. It was important to her that we all, black and white, understand this important but less known literature.

I read *Soul on Ice* for a book report. At 15, I found Eldridge Cleaver's theories on race and gender startling in their strangeness and bluntness. Even now I remember thinking Cleaver's analogy of the Holy Trinity to 3-in-One oil was smart, but his observations of the significance of Lynda Bird Johnson doing the Watusi (a popular dance in the 1960s) overblown. One sentence that I did find wise: "The price of hating other human beings is loving oneself less." (8). I doubt I would have read *Soul on Ice* if I had not been in that teacher's class and at Hillside.

I was impressed by the way small things mattered to this teacher. One day I saw her bend down to pick a pencil off the floor and put it in her pocket. A seemingly unremarkable gesture, but it was so characteristic of her way of finding everything useful and of value—even what others might throw away. My geometry teacher also was a white woman, but even younger, and tall, with long, straight dark brown hair (like mine at that time). It is easy for me to imagine her in jeans and sandals outside school, but she dressed like a grown-up for teaching. She was serious about math and a good teacher. She was thoughtful about her job and fair to everyone. After a few weeks, she gave me and about five other students, black and white, boys and girls, the opportunity to do geometry as an independent study class. We went to the library and worked proofs most days, coming into the class to take tests when they were scheduled. I was thrilled. To be recognized for my abilities and to have the chance to work ahead and not feel like I was wasting time in class was affirming.

Biology was a required class, and my teacher was a small, dark brown man with short hair and a mustache. He always wore a suit and tie. He was a little odd; some said he was shell-shocked from World War II. Sometimes I could not understand what he was saying—it sounded like he was mumbling—and his teaching was a bit scattered, but he was a nice man. Students took advantage of him, though, lying about why they did not have their assignments completed or had missed a class.

I remember three things from his class: my mad crush on my biology partner, Tony; that I dissected a frog, which was pretty yucky; and that I learned about contraception—which we called "birth control"—from a nurse from the health department (something that was very useful to me later). It may be surprising that contraception was taught in a matter-of-fact way in school then, because it is so controversial now. But at the time, knowledge of contraception was considered practical information for students. There were girls at Hillside who had babies at home (though there were no obviously pregnant girls at school). Educators believed providing the correct information to students could reduce unwanted pregnancies. And it probably did.

I took art from an older black teacher, slightly balding with white hair, an artist himself who had been at Hillside a long time. Art also was a part of my identity—on my own I drew, quilted (as did both my grandmothers), block printed, and crocheted. In this class, we worked with various media. We had little formal instruction from the teacher. We talked about the works of some artists, such as one of his favorite black painters, Romare Bearden, but most of our time was unstructured while we worked on projects. I kept a sketchbook for class, which I also wrote things in, sort of like a journal, including some poetry. I still do this as an adult.

I took physical education only in my sophomore year. We had two PE teachers for the girls—a short white woman and a tall black woman. We had terrible gym uniforms—one-piece, dark blue outfits that snapped up the front with elastic around the legs. I took PE only because it was a requirement. I tried hard to lose myself in the back row of our large class so no one would call on me to do anything. Believing myself to be terrible at sports, I wanted to just melt into the scenery until the gym period was over.

* * *

Students from four junior high schools fed into the newly integrated Hillside High School, two predominantly black schools—Whitted and Shepard (LaHoma's new school and her old school) and two predominantly white schools—my Rogers-Herr and Holton. I knew something of both Whitted and Shepard because we had competed against them in football, basketball and baseball. I had never thought about how these schools might be different from each other, however, and I never heard anyone talk about it, either. In my mind, they both had just been black junior high schools.

Rogers-Herr and Holton both had predominantly white student populations before the desegregation plan, but Rogers-Herr students thought of themselves as being very different from Holton students. We considered Holton, located in East Durham, a "redneck" school, and Holton students thought Rogers-Herr students were "stuck-up." There were few if any, friendships between Rogers-Herr kids and Holton kids before coming to Hillside, and only a few afterward.

* * *

I realized my sophomore year that one of the best things about being at Hillside was that it liberated us from much of the influence of social class that had caused me so much grief in junior high school. At least it liberated me from caring about it as much. Some of the students whose parents were at the highest rung of the social ladder at Rogers-Herr had left public schools and gone on to prep school, and others left in their junior and senior years. All the rest of us had been dumped into an existing school culture that tolerated us but did not need us much. Where any of the white people fit in vis-a-vis each other was of little concern to most of the student body. Having been popular in junior high school was of little consequence at Hillside.

Racial quotas were imposed for some activities, but it was a much more level playing field for white students than it had been at Rogers-Herr. If anything, we all were at the same disadvantage in this new place. Cheerleading and band at Hillside, for example, had longstanding traditions that reflected a black culture unfamiliar to us. Being popular in junior high school was not helpful in getting on the cheerleading squads. Quotas ensured some white faces, but we recognized that the white girls who made the squad were affirmative-action cases and were not the same caliber of cheerleaders as the black girls, who knew what it meant to be a Hillside Hornet. The white girls had a steep learning curve when it came to the more soulful traditional Hillside-style cheers, in sync with the band's "blacker" music.

* * *

My friends and I went to most of the football games and got to see our friend, one of the white girls who made the squad, cheerlead. While there were white students in the band and cheerleading, there were few white football players. All high schools in Durham played their football games at Durham's County Stadium in northern Durham, a neutral location acceptable to my parents for extracurricular activities. Though I never loved the game itself, I enjoyed the spectacle, especially the Hillside marching band's half-time show. Their syncopated movement ("stepping") to music was so much better than the routines of any of the bands from the white schools. We saw and talked to our black classmates at the games, but we never socialized outside the stadium.

* * *

In school, I began to learn about a middle-class black culture. Most of what I had seen about black life on television was through the news shows, primarily focused on the poverty of black life or related to civil-rights struggles that often turned violent. I had thought most differences between black and white cultures were related to differences in resources. For example, I expected poor black people (who lived in ghettos) to speak differently than white people because of their isolation from white people and their lack of education. A common "complaint" among white people was that they could not understand what poor black people were saying.

Primetime television series rarely spotlighted black characters when I was in junior high and high school, but when they did, they were characters firmly assimilated into white culture: Bill Cosby in *I Spy*, Lincoln Hayes in *The Mod Squad*, Julia in the show of the same name. Television shows depicting middle or upper-class black families—*What's Happening!!*, *A Different World* and the like—did not appear until after I graduated from high school. I expected the educated black people I was around at Hillside would speak more or less like white people all the time. And they did, more or less, but not always.

Many of the educated black people with whom I spoke at Hillside had been educated in mostly black settings, and there were some differences in their speech that interested me. The black teachers pronounced "Aunt" "aahnt" while my white friends and I said "ant." Black adults at school and students also added a second syllable when pronouncing the name for the letter "r." Instead of one syllable, it became two, saying "r-ra." This was not evident in specific words, just in how the name of the letter was pronounced, unless the word ended in an r. For example, I heard my black teachers pronounce the word "car" as "car-ra." I thought it was so odd that I had never heard it before—certainly not in conversations between (white-assimilated) black people I had heard on television or in movies. It was my first inkling that black life, even middle-class black life, could go on without full assimilation into white life, and probably preferred to do so.

The rest of the cultural difference is a bit harder to describe, but there was a greater formality between teachers and students and among adults also than I had experienced in my white world, even my Southern white world that has its own code of whom to call "ma'am" and "sir." There seemed to be more social space between black students and teachers, even among the teachers themselves, and certainly a greater hierarchy among teachers and administrators based on age and experience. Greetings and salutations were longer; people took more time to get to the heart of the conversation because there were a lot of words spoken to establish relationships with one another. There was more "small talk" at the beginning of a conversation to give everyone time to relax and understand how each one in the conversation was doing. Efficiency was not the point of communication; creating relationship was.

I appreciate this use of language now as an adult, though at the time, I was secretly annoyed with this formality. I had some judgment about it; it seemed a bit to me like putting on "airs." I was used to some of the small talk and storytelling Southerners use in their casual conversations with one another, but in these black conversations it seemed somehow different. I was shy and self-conscious in my conversations with those I did not know well. I might have felt some anxiety about not knowing the rules of how to engage in this kind of dialogue. I'm sure I was concerned about possible missteps between my elders and me. My unconscious white privilege turned this anxiety into irritation.

Another cultural difference I noticed was about appearance. It was the '70s, and white boys and girls dressed informally, usually in jeans. The black girls put much more time and effort into their appearance, "dressing up" more than the white girls. They were more likely to wear dresses and stockings and heels, to use makeup and spend more time with their hair. I think this was the same for black teachers compared to white teachers.

* * *

In addition to going to football games, my school friends and I carried on the same out-of-school activities together in high school as in junior high school, some school-related, most not—shopping, movies, birthday parties, just hanging out. Our sophomore year, we were still dependent on our parents to drive us places, so we were limited in what we could do. My parents' concern about the safety of the neighborhood near Hillside ruled out going to basketball games and dances at school. Even afternoon activities after school were discouraged. Extracurricular activities that might have broadened my social life became a casualty of desegregation.

Social events in my all-white church were closer to home and thus easier to participate in, an important part of the white world I lived in outside of my school day. I was still in Sunday school, youth choir, and youth group. At church, I became friends with Joan and Cathy and another Lynn, but they went to a predominantly white county school. My church friends were more interested in doing well in school, and their tastes in clothes, music, and movies were closer to mine than were those of my school friends. We also had a common bond of belief that connected us in a more spiritual and emotional way than my connection with my school friends.

* * *

Boys became a focus of attention during our sophomore year.

I had an awkward few dates between ninth and 10th grades with the brother of a friend at school. Rather than saying I wasn't interested in getting romantic, I was not so nice to him, hoping he wouldn't ask me out again. And he didn't. It was unusual for me not to acquiesce, but being difficult on purpose was easier than being honest about not liking him. That's the socially awkward person I was at 15.

The field of date-able boys for me at Hillside—that is to say, white boys—was relatively small. The few boys I dated in high school had gone to Holton, and for the most part I did not consider them to be on the same academic wavelength as I was. Spending time with them felt awkward because I had little in common with them intellectually, which translated into not having much to keep us going conversationally. The boys I did feel intellectually equal to, most of whom had gone to my junior high school, did not date much. Of course, in adolescence, there are more than intellectual interests at work.

My earlier-mentioned lab partner on whom I had a hard crush was a boy who had gone to Holton. He had deep brown eyes with long eyelashes, a great smile, blond (peroxided) hair with a bit of a curl in it. I sat beside him every day in biology, in the deep lust of a hormone-oozing 15-year-old. He drove a very cool redneck car—a dark maroon Comet, with a loud air-scoop and jacked-up wheels. Cars were his passion, and I talked to him—or rather listened to him talk—about his as if I cared about it. He was kind of a bad boy, a "hood" (as opposed to being "from the 'hood'"). He also seemed troubled a lot, tired, and (I realize as an adult) probably hung over. I tried to be sympathetic and covered for him when necessary. He called me on the phone sometimes, but he never asked me out; I never really expected that he would, though I hoped. And girls did not ask boys out—ever. I found out later he still had a girlfriend in junior high school at Holton.

* * *

My musical tastes in high school were mainstream white and female. I liked folk music. I owned albums by James Taylor, Carole King, Elton John, Rod Stewart, Joni Mitchell, and Judy Collins. I listened to a lot of AM radio. I had friends who sang and played guitar. After hearing it at school, I listened to a lot of soul music, too—Aretha Franklin, The Temptations, Jackson 5 and Gladys Knight. The "Theme From Shaft" opened many of our assemblies. I liked the way people might get up and dance during a pep rally or an assembly when there was music that moved them, though I would never do that myself. It was not a white thing; only black kids did that.

One of the out-of-school highlights of my sophomore year was going to my first stadium concert to hear James Taylor and Carole King at Dorton Arena in Raleigh. I went with my friend Joan from church and her older sister, who drove us. It cost $15, which I saved up for out of my babysitting money (I made 50 cents an hour). James Taylor sang everything from his recently released Sweet Baby James album. Carole King sang everything from her soon-to-be released *Tapestry* album. I was so elated about this evening out (on a school night!) that not even my mother's grumpiness about the smell of cigarette smoke from the concert lingering in my long hair and clothing could dampen my mood.

* * *

Every summer my family spent time in Waynesville, a small town in the North Carolina mountains, where my grandparents lived and where my parents had built a vacation/retirement house. Any time we spent there was more than either my brother or I wanted, however, as we would rather be with our friends back home.

When we were in Durham, I spent as much time as I could with my church friends. We helped with a summer recreation program for elementary school children several mornings a week, went to watch the men's softball team compete in a church league and ended the summer with church camp at Camp Kanata.

In my post-sophomore summer, I turned 16. I was able to take driver's education class and get my license—a serious rite of passage among my peers. My church friends arranged a memorable surprise birthday party for me, blindfolding me and driving me to Chapel Hill to the Zoom Zoom, one of our favorite restaurants. Because of this birthday, however, I had another rite of passage to fulfill. It weighed heavily on me that I was sweet 16 but had never been kissed. I was not pursuing anyone, but I felt I was missing something. Toward the end of the summer, I got an unexpected call from my biology partner Tony, asking if he could visit me that afternoon. I managed to speak over the thumping of my heart, "Yes, that would be great."

I then briefed my mother on the situation in a way that would communicate my desire for privacy without arousing suspicion and rushed to my room to change into my most alluring blouse.

His jacked-up Comet roared up my otherwise calm street and stopped in front of my house. And there he was, from the other side of town, standing on my front porch, curly blond hair, twinkling eyes, and lovely smile. We sat in the living room on the floor in front of the couch. My mother was around the corner in the kitchen—amazingly, she didn't interrupt us the whole time. We talked for about an hour—about what I have no idea. I'm sure I was barely breathing.

Before he left, he reached over, and he kissed me—a sweet, soft, passionate kiss. And then he was gone. Period. Forever. Never to be seen again. What I learned later from school gossip was that the girlfriend I had not known about had gotten pregnant. (Where was he the day the lady from the health department came to talk about contraception? Probably skipping class.) He had decided that summer to quit school—a detail not mentioned before our kiss—and he got a job and married his pregnant girlfriend in the fall.

Tony was part of a secret self that I did not share with others, possibly for fear of disapproval. He was not the type of boy I was supposed to like. I never told my friends about my crush on him or told them about the kiss. But in that moment I did not know it would be the last time I would see him, and I felt exhilarated. I had had a great first kiss with a beautiful boy.

Junior Year (1971-1972)

The big news during our junior year was a rule change that allowed us to go off campus for lunch. I did not have a car, so my leaving required finding people who did. Though it was rare, sometimes I'd have to skip a class because of a late return from lunch. My fear of being an object of Mr. Alston's attention kept me on campus most lunch times.

Mr. Alston was the assistant principal, the principal's right-hand man. The old guard Hillsiders called him "Prof" Alston. He had been at Hillside many years, beginning as a chemistry teacher. He was probably in his 50s, 6 feet tall, light brown and thin. Always in a suit and tie, with glasses on a mostly bald head. He had a powerful voice that carried down the hallways. He was well loved in the black, Hillside community, but I wasn't part of that community and could not understand, try as I might, why people liked him so much.

He made me nervous, and I worked hard to keep myself out of his sights. He was very different from other (white) school administrators I had known. There were people he kept an eye on, even if they did not seem to be causing trouble, and he called them out in public whenever he could. He walked the halls constantly and often had a posse of students he had found skipping class following him around.

I think some of my reaction to him was because he was part of the black Hillside culture that was unfamiliar to me. There was just a different quality in the way he engaged people that seemed threatening to me, but not threatening to black students who had known about Mr. Alston all their lives as part of their community. His way of calling students out may have been to make people feel as though someone cared about their presence. I, on the other hand, wanted no attention from any disciplinarian. I didn't feel comfortable making small talk with him, nor did I know when he just was kidding around.

Disciplinary measures at Hillside when I was there were so much gentler than what I hear about at schools now. We had dress codes at school—boys were not to wear hats in the building, and there were rules about how short girls' skirts could be and how much midriff could show. No flip-flops. Jeans were fine; I wore them a lot. I dressed like a hippie, though I wasn't part of the mostly white hippie-ish clique.

There were some instances of misbehavior in class, people talking, coming in late, not having done their homework. It was all the usual stuff you expect from high school students. I was nearly always in college-prep classes, which meant greater motivation to be there, less boredom or resentment or whatever causes people to misbehave. Black teachers and white teachers handled discipline similarly in classes I was in—some combination of shaming by being called out in front of others ("Is this the way a young lady is supposed to act?") and taking away lunch privileges. The bigger offenses were being out of class or off campus when it was not allowed or without a pass. Punishments were not severe; there were no suspensions, in-class or otherwise. Nothing was so disruptive it required police intervention.

Parental fears for the safety of white students in a black school turned out to be unfounded at Hillside. There were no guns or knives at school and no Officer Friendly (or not so friendly) walking his/her beat. I heard of only a few fights, and those were not racially motivated. Our principal, Mr. Lucas (later Dr. Lucas), had been at Hillside since 1962, and the community and the teachers trusted him. There had been a discussion of transferring him to Durham High School as part of the desegregation plan the year before, but I am thankful he stayed at Hillside High School. I did not always agree with every decision he made while I was a student there, but with 20/20 (adult) hindsight I understand that much of the reason for the tranquility of the desegregation effort at Hillside was because of Mr. Lucas. He was a trusted part of the black community before desegregation, and he was able to win over the trust of white parents and students who were new to the school.

* * *

My junior year I took American literature, American history, algebra 2 (trigonometry), French 3, chemistry, and art. I also studied for and took the PSAT and my first SAT. Most of my teachers that year, as it turned out, were white, though mostly just by chance.

My science and math teachers were both female and white. Chemistry was my biggest challenge. My 30-something teacher was smart and straightforward and fair, but my brain did not get chemistry. We sat at tables of four, and thank goodness I had no crushes on anyone sitting at my table, or I might have had an even harder time of it.

My algebra 2 teacher was short and had shoulder-length brown hair sometimes pulled back into a ponytail. She had a broad, often-smiling face. She was young, not long out of college. Although she taught math, she saw her mission as expanding our minds regarding politics and social-justice issues. She often used class time to express her views on current events, including the Vietnam War. She wore leather sandals and flowing dresses. She was critical of the school administration for various reasons, spoke her mind and, according to her, was in trouble a lot with the school administration when she disagreed with school policy. I liked her; I admired her rebel spirit but was a bit too timid to follow her lead. I wanted to be a rebel but was always a little too nervous about the consequences.

My French teacher for my first two years at Hillside was a woman who had gone to Hillside as a student herself and spoke French with a Southern black accent. She was less than 5 feet tall, though she always wore high heels, so she stood taller. She wore her jewelry big and her curly hair short. Our lessons were a mix of conversation practice and French literature; the plays by Moliere were what I enjoyed most. I made good grades on written tests but was not pushed hard to speak French well. I liked her, but I was worried I was not getting the best language education.

Mr. Alston, the nemesis of my imagination, would pop into various classes, stop what was happening and randomly ask students questions that might not have anything to do with the topic being taught. He started teaching chemistry at Hillside after he returned from serving in World War II, and before becoming the dean of boys, he had taught some of the teachers now at Hillside, including my French teacher. Mr. Alston would come into her class with a piece of paper with French sentences written on it; he would write those sentences on the board and ask students to translate. When he came in, she would let him take over.

At that point, I would roll my eyes and silently sigh. I thought it was silly and a waste of time. I was worried he would call on me, and I would have no idea what he had written on the board, and, worse than that, he would remember me the next time he saw me in the hall and make me walk around with him.

I also took typing one semester of my junior year. We used manual typewriters. It was the most practical skill I learned in high school, very useful in college, where I made a little extra money typing people's papers. I still type faster than most people. Almost all of the students in the class were female, both black and white. Contrary to type (at least to my mind and no pun intended), the teacher was a young man.

* * *

There were no cell phones or email or texts when I was in high school. (Thank goodness!) When I was waiting for a boy to call me at home, I sat by my family's black rotary phone on the red desk in our tiny kitchen. Girls did not call boys, ever. Through the first part of my junior year, most of the calls for me were from girlfriends from school or church or from people asking me to babysit.

Sometime in early spring of my junior year, our phone began to ring with some regularity with calls from Mitch, a senior boy with whom I eventually started going steady. He was a few inches taller than I and had brown hair with sideburns and serious blue eyes. He was a nice guy but a little over the top in sometimes embarrassing ways.

Mitch had a full-time job after school and drove a royal blue Volkswagen bug. He took me out on weekends and bought me flowers more often than seemed appropriate. Because we were allowed to go off campus for lunch, I spent many lunch hours making out with him in his small car on the backside of Forest Hills Park. It was fun to have a boyfriend. When he asked me to go steady, I said "yes," and I wore his big fat class ring with white tape wrapped around it so it would stay on my finger. He started going with me to my church.

Mitch's family life and upbringing were different from mine. He was from East Durham and had gone to Holton. His parents were both deceased, and he lived with his aunt. I'm not sure what happened to his father, but his mother had been killed in a car accident while she was driving intoxicated down the wrong way on a highway ramp. He had several half brothers and sisters. He had a history of getting intensely involved with girls and then dumping them unexpectedly. This last fact I learned too late.

I enjoyed his attention and was sympathetic with his family story, but I was sometimes embarrassed by his social behavior. I was uncomfortable listening to his relatives' racist conversations when visiting Mitch's brother and his aunt and uncle in their homes and at their evangelical church out in the country. Out of politeness to my hosts, I did not say anything (although I did not join in). Mitch knew better and did not join in when I was there, but I got the feeling he might have otherwise.

My school and church friends accepted Mitch when he was with me, but he would not have been part of our group otherwise. The working/middle class I was part of had its own rules and expectations, mostly about education and aspiration. His life was more chaotic than mine, and his family less educated. College was not part of his family script. Although I felt like a snob to think those things, I did think them, and at the same time, I was glad for his affection. The aura of teenage sexuality that enveloped us as a couple made my mother very nervous. Mitch and I did a lot of making out and heavy petting, although we never "went all the way." I enjoyed it and felt guilty about that. I had no one to talk to, though, for fear of judgment from my girlfriends, especially my church friends, so sex was another part of my secret self. To be clear, I'm not sure what they would have said. No one talked about sex, so I just assumed they'd disapprove.

Several of my friends were also in serious relationships our junior year, the most notable of which was another "mixed" Rogers-Herr and Holton relationship between my friend Beth and Ricky. We knew Ricky in class because he was part of a few of the students who had come from Holton who were in college prep classes. Beth was beautiful but shy, and Ricky was cute, drove a cool car and was not shy at all. One smart, intense boy from Rogers-Herr, a year ahead of us, was smitten with Beth and wooed her tenaciously, but the more carefree Ricky won her over. He became part of our group of friends (and Beth part of his), so that he was our primary entrée into East Durham and Holton kids—more so than Mitch, who was so busy working after school that he didn't have a lot of close friends.

Interracial dating did not occur frequently at Hillside while I was there. I heard about one interracial couple rumored to be dating my junior year (I'm sure there was more than one). Both were athletes, and it seems the rumors were likely to have been true, but the relationship was short-lived. All the interracial couples I knew about—including the athlete couple—were black boys and white girls. No black boys ever asked me out. There might have been an athlete or two whom I found attractive, but I never entertained the possibility. I did not think my parents would have approved if asked, but there was no reason to ask, and so I do not know for sure.

* * *

Mitch and I talked about going to the prom my junior year—he was a senior—but I thought my parents would not allow me to go, and I did not ask them. I never went to any dance at Hillside, partly because I did not date much. A greater reason was my parents' concerns about being in a different neighborhood at night and, again, their fears that underlying racial tensions could erupt—probably even more likely in the wake of possible intimate contact. (And, was this not the real fear behind all of it?)

I don't know how many white couples went to the dances—some I am sure—or what it was like for them. My close friends did not go. If they had, I might have tried harder to persuade my parents to let me go. Though I had looked forward to dances as part of my high school experience, that was not to be.

Although none of my girlfriends had her own car, we were all allowed to drive our families' cars most places we wanted to go. We always drove ourselves to Young Life—a weekly gathering, organized by school affiliation, that was loosely Christian and, in Durham, led by Duke University students. The gatherings were not held at school but rather at different people's houses. Always white people's houses, always close to my neighborhood, definitely a predominantly white crowd but not exclusively so. Young Life was an activity in which it was possible for my friends and me to hang out with a wider group of people than we normally did and listen to cool college students (i.e., cute guys) talk about Jesus. Usually, there was a guitar and singing. It was Jesus-lite, nothing too heavy, a nice vibe and more than anything a place for students to socialize after school during the week without getting into trouble.

I also was influenced by evangelists who ran large, nondenominational youth revivals that came to Durham. They were young and hip, and the talk was more about spiritual liberation and social justice than the fundamentalism that people today equate with Christianity. These revivals occurred at the beginning of what became Christian folk and rock music, and I wanted to be part of it. "Getting high on Jesus" felt like a real thing. I am not sure I would have called myself a Jesus freak, but it would have been an apt label.

* * *

Feminism, known as "women's liberation" in those days, also spoke to me when I was in high school. I was smart (if self-effacing), and I had no question that I could compete with men in most ways. I was not athletic and was never going to compete with men physically, but that was the least of it. Many smart female teachers at school helped me see what might be possible in my life that perhaps had not been possible for my mother's generation. I also babysat for women who were in feminist consciousness-raising groups. They loaned me such books as *The Feminine Mystique* and *Sisterhood Is Powerful*. They were going through divorces and otherwise negotiating their way into this new reality. I admired them, but I secretly was glad I was younger than they were so the world would be "fixed" by the time I got out of college.

I had some serious arguments with my father about my feminist ideas. I did not have the vocabulary that people use now about equity and equality, and I felt inarticulate during my angry arguments with my father. How could the parent who I thought was my best advocate say it was OK—in general—for women to have limited opportunities in life? It made no sense that the man who had always expected me to go to college could argue against equal protection for women under the law.

I dissolved into tears during one heated discussion, to which Daddy responded, "Crying, just like a woman." I was infuriated and confused about this disconnect between his support for me and his more general sexist attitudes. I was to learn as I grew up that this inconsistency between the personal and the abstract is not rare—and certainly relevant to attitudes about race as well.

My mother never espoused a feminist ideology, but she thought women should be recognized for the work they did well. Though she agreed with the Equal Rights Amendment, she certainly did not identify as a feminist. One time as we were driving home from Hillside I declared I did not want to be a "stay at home mom," or a "Suzy Homemaker." Mother did not say anything, just acted hurt. I didn't apologize; I just pretended I didn't know I had just belittled her.

* * *

At the close of the year, I was a junior marshal for the graduation ceremony. It was Mitch's graduation, and we celebrated at dinner with some of his family. That summer, I worked again in the church recreation program, and I spent three weeks at a Baptist youth conference with my church friend Lynn and then took a long road trip with my family. While I was away, Mitch surprised me by applying to and getting into N.C. State University. His earlier plans had been to go to the local community college. I was glad he was going to college, but I knew it would change our relationship.

Senior Year: 1972-1973

My senior year started with Mitch breaking up with me. Though it was, in truth, good for me and a bit of a relief, no one likes to get dumped. I was used to having him around and was sad and embarrassed no longer to be part of a couple. After several bad blind dates that fall, I resigned myself to the idea that I would have to wait until I got to college to meet the man of my dreams.

* * *

Academically, I was getting myself ready for college. Though math was not my strong suit, I took a third year of math, which was then called "analysis" and was taught by the same teacher who had taught me sophomore geometry as an independent study. This time I stayed in her class, hanging on to whatever I could learn from her.

Little of the content of the world history class I took from an assistant football coach my senior year lingers in my memory. He was white, young, but starting to bald and trying to be gruff, wanting us to think he was macho but having a bit of a soft spot for his students. What I remember best from that class, though, was a different sort of lesson about my fellow students.

During one class, we went to the library to do some research, and I sat at a table with some black, sophomore girls (there were students from all grade levels in this class) I did not know except in class. They were all talking about their babies at home—their names, how old they were, who was taking care of them. I knew there were girls at school who were mothers, but these girls were all sophomores, and there were four or five of them in this one class. Too late for the contraception lecture in sophomore biology! I could not imagine trying to keep up with school and having a baby at home—I felt so naïve about the realities of some of my classmates' lives but also grateful for whatever had kept me from being in their situation at that age.

I also took European literature my senior year. Literature was always a favorite subject for me, as it was a way to understand the personal and social world. My teacher was a delicate woman the color of café au lait, with hair in loose curls close to her head. She was slender and wore clothing with ruffles and floral designs—a little old-fashioned in my opinion, but still flattering on her. She had a sweet, thin voice that she did not raise even when the class became boisterous; instead, she would just lightly tap her pen on the desk when she wanted our attention. She had attended Hillside as a student. Her softness was a cause for student amusement and parody and, although I felt bad about the way people made fun of her, I sometimes joined in the mimicry.

Two works of literature come to mind when I think of her— *Macbeth* and *A Dolls' House*. We read both those plays aloud in class, with different people taking different parts. I can hear her playing the female lead in *A Dolls' House*, calling, "Torvald!" Ibsen's drama about a woman who sought to free herself from her husband's power over her life made an impression on me as I was beginning to think about my future life choices.

Psychology was taught as a social-studies subject my senior year, and I was excited to take it. The teacher who had the most direct influence on my academic career taught it. She was a young white woman but had not come to Hillside directly from college. She had been in the Peace Corps, among other things, before teaching. I had already had her for American history my junior year and liked her very much.

She had grown up in a white, liberal Southern family, but her college education and life since then had been in Boston and New York, so she brought an intellectual, urban vibe with her. Social studies as a discipline provided a lot of opportunities for questioning the status quo and for critical thinking—including issues related to race and gender and power. She was up to the task of making us think about complex subjects.

Her white skin was pale, almost porcelain. She was not shy but spoke softly in a sing-songy kind of way that caused some students to erroneously call her "Silly S____." I seldom spoke in her class (or anyone else's), but I listened intently. Kind and fair, she tried from time to time to pull me into the discussion. She asked me to teach a class on the book *Future Shock* by Alvin Toffler—a best seller at the time. She met with me to discuss what I was going to say and told me she had been a typist for Mr. Toffler in New York. I was impressed and amazed that I knew someone who knew a famous author.

This teacher showed me a bigger world than the one I was thinking of for myself. I had always thought I'd be a teacher, but I found myself in psychology. It resonated with my interest in how people make sense of the world around them. A new academic path opened up to me.

I had a new French teacher my senior year, somewhat plain looking, with brown frizzy hair, shirtwaist dresses, sensible shoes, and glasses. Russian by birth and with a heavy Russian accent, she was very dramatic, with great *joie de vivre*. She sometimes waltzed around the room, playing all the parts from Moliere's *Le Malade Imaginaire*. I am grateful to her for making Moliere, Rimbaud, and Camus come alive. Reading *La Symphonie Pastorale* by Andre Gide for her class opened a major fissure in my religious beliefs that took decades for me to work through. Examining the complexities of life even if they are uncomfortable is what I believe constitutes a good education.

In that class, we had a young student teacher from France who taught us that the French colonizers made African children learn by rote the same things French children learn, such as *Je suis un Gaulois*, when plainly they were not descendants of the Roman Empire. That was my introduction to the tyranny of language.

Some students said classes at Hillside were so easy they never had to study; I was not sure how that was possible. I may not have worked as hard as my church friends at their whiter county high school, but I studied hard, did my homework and wrote papers to make A's.

Though I had an intrinsic love of reading and learning, I was competitive about grades throughout high school, finishing fifth in my class at graduation. My SAT scores went up about 100 points the second time I took the test my senior year. I made good grades because I knew how to give teachers what they wanted without any pushback, and I was a good test-taker. My competitiveness about grades probably came from not being athletic and being self-conscious around boys—except when it came to academics. I was artistic, but I did not have much of an outlet for recognition as an artist, so intellectual pursuits were where I got self-esteem.

* * *

The only alcohol I ever imbibed in high school was in the context of an assignment. A classmate and I made a rum and Coke while we were making a *Bouche de Noel* for a French class Christmas party, with rum being one of the ingredients. There was not enough rum to get even the smallest buzz, but it made me nervous, and I decided I would just wait until I was in college and did not have to deal with my parent's disapproval of alcohol before I tried drinking again.

I knew about drugs in high school, but I was not that interested, and it just seemed that if I were going to experiment at all, I would wait until my parents were not monitoring my every move. I knew people who smoked pot and used other kinds of drugs, but none of my close friends at school or church did, so there was no peer pressure. And, anyway, I was getting high on Jesus! I heard that drugs were bought and sold at school, but I had no personal knowledge of any of that.

As strange as it seems to me now, students were allowed to smoke cigarettes at school. Smoking in class was not permitted, but there was a designated space for students to smoke outside, under a covered walkway between buildings, known as the "smoking corral." The smoking corral was one place my sophomore year where I could get a glimpse of Tony, my lab partner, outside of class, so sometimes that year I passed by there just in case.

* * *

My maternal grandmother, who lived in the North Carolina mountains where my mother had grown up, died of breast cancer in February of my senior year. Mother's grief over my grandmother's death lasted a long time and had a dampening effect on the second half of my senior year. I loved my grandmother, but we had not been close. I had a harder time dealing with my mother's sadness than my own. Mother cried a lot and sang my grandmother's favorite hymns around the house. With no appetite after her mother's death, Mother lost weight and then started worrying that she was dying, that she had cancer, too. She repeatedly went to the doctor to find out what was wrong, until she developed a hiatal hernia, possibly from the anxiety. Mother's depression finally lifted after she had a medical diagnosis and treatment.

I felt as if I were going crazy, too. I experienced a lot of "free-floating anxiety"—something was wrong, but I could not figure out what it was. It felt like guilt but was not guilt exactly; it was a bad feeling that something was askew and I did not know how to make it right. Eventually, the feeling lifted, but it was scary at the time. I never told anyone about it until years later in therapy.

* * *

I applied to two universities my senior year and got into both. I applied to the first, Wake Forest University, only because my guidance counselor made me. The other, the University of North Carolina at Chapel Hill (UNC) was easily my first choice. UNC was less expensive, and it was also closer to my heart. Judith got in also, and we decided to room together.

After we had received our early admission letters, Judith and I went over to campus with our mothers to look at dorms. Co-ed dorms were a new phenomenon around the country and at UNC. There was one group of co-ed dorms on North Campus, the area where we wanted to live. I thought it sounded interesting, but our mothers were not thrilled. Mother had us talk to Annie Queen, a friend of hers from Waynesville, who had gone to Berea College in Kentucky and then had been the head of the Campus Y at UNC for many years. We sat in her cute cottage house close to campus and drank tea from pottery mugs while she graciously talked to us about various dorms and gave us advice about college. Ultimately, we decided on the all-women Cobb Dorm, centrally located on North Campus and not too far from several boys' dorms and most of our classrooms.

Springtime stretched out endlessly while we waited to graduate. In addition to the malaise I associated with my grandmother's death and my mother's grief, French existentialism was causing the first small cracks in my Christian faith. I had an intense discussion walking home from Duke Gardens during spring break with my church friend Lynn (who also had read Gide's *La Symphonie Pastorale*) about what seemed to be some inconsistencies in the faith we then professed, as pointed out through the book's story of a wayward priest. This was not yet a full-blown dismantling, but it was making me nervous.

Graduation finally came. Of an initial sophomore class of 500 students, about 300 of us graduated, with the others having moved away or dropped out. Graduation was always at County Stadium. Mickey Michaux spoke, a Hillside graduate who had just started his political career as a representative in the N.C. General Assembly (where he is still in office). After lots of hugs and congratulations with my friends, I went home with my parents.

Some of my friends went to the beach for a few days after graduation. I didn't because I was nervous about the kinds of trouble my friends might get into with drinking, and I was shy about being with larger groups of kids. And I did not have a boyfriend. The post-beach story was that girls who had boyfriends slept with them there, which would seem like no news now but was significant at the time.

I spent the rest of the summer babysitting and hanging out with (mostly) church friends. I was eager to get on with college and, more important, to experience the new freedoms of being away from home, even if the distance was only a dozen miles down the road.

I felt finished with Hillside when I graduated. Being white at Hillside had not been a bad experience for me—not at all. If anything, my time there was notable for its ordinariness. There had been nothing to fear regarding safety. I had never felt afraid. My friends were mostly the same ones I entered high school with, plus a few boyfriends who joined our group. I may have left worried about my competitiveness in college, but I also had learned a lot. I knew my experience had been different than if I had gone to Durham High School. I was sure I knew more about black history, literature, art, and music than I might have otherwise. I had learned that there was a whole black working/middle class culture that was not portrayed in the media, and that it was possible for people to live in separate realities even in the same physical spaces. These realizations may have been the greatest gift my time at Hillside gave to me.

I continued to believe that integrated schools were part of a process of creating better relationships among people of different races. As I was leaving Hillside that spring of 1973, it seemed reasonable to assume that racially integrated schools would be the norm everywhere at some time in the not-so-distant future, and that we had just been part of the first wave. I felt satisfied to have been part of that change and pleased that I had done what was asked of me to help make the world better for everyone. But now I was going to college where some of the pressure was off, and I could relax around the issue of race. Being white meant that it was possible for me to do that.

Cindy Waszak, Senior Portrait.

SEVEN

Finally at Hillside:
It's All About the Band

LaHoma

My struggles for independence from my parents continued, but my transition from junior high to high school was made easier for one essential reason: the marching band. This was no ordinary group of musicians. The Hillside Marching Hornets were the most talented, baddest band in the land. I knew they were world famous (at least to us), and no other high school in the area had the reputation or following of the Hillside band. As a young black Durhamite, I used to look forward to seeing three things during the holiday parades: Hillside High Band, North Carolina Central University band and Santa Claus. My affection for Santa Claus soon faded, but my love of the bands never wavered.

The majorettes leading the band seemed to me to be the prettiest girls, with beautiful long brown legs. They could twirl and catch their batons and dance in perfect coordination with the cadence of the drummers. Then the band would play a familiar tune, belted out with confidence. How I loved Hillside's band! I began to dream that I, too, one day, could be in that band.

One of the reasons I persevered with the French horn in the eighth grade was that I thought it might help me get into the marching band at Hillside. But I had two problems. One was that I could not see myself playing and lugging around the French horn in the marching band, especially given the complex dance routines the band was known for. And second, I really wanted to be a majorette.

But therein lay two more problems: First, I did not know how to twirl a baton. Second, that year the band director, Mr. Edgerton, required that anyone who tried out for the majorette squad had to play an instrument at least her first year—sophomore year—in the marching band. He also had a large squad of seniors, so he was not selecting any sophomores that year to be a majorette. What was an aspiring majorette to do?

My quick solution was to take flute lessons. I picked the flute, not because I thought that it was the easiest instrument, but because it was the lightest. So, while my classmates were planning to try out for Hillside's band using instruments they'd been playing for at least two years, I started taking lessons on a completely new instrument that I had to master in a few weeks.

I convinced my parents to buy me a second-hand flute. Then I coaxed some of my peers to show me what they knew. I bought a beginner's book, and basically taught myself how to play the flute in the last few weeks of the ninth grade and before summer band tryouts. I could read sheet music and learned just enough to play the major notes and chords, and somehow convinced myself that I played well enough to sit for auditions. Luckily they were group auditions, which went well enough for me to gain a spot in the marching band. Either Mr. Edgerton felt I had some potential or he just felt sorry for me, but either way, I did it, I made the band!

I was never any good at playing the flute, but I managed to avoid attracting attention by pretending to be really engaged and also by playing very softly. My saving grace was that I could read sheet music very well, so I could chime in loudly at the end of the stanza, or I memorized a few chords well enough to hit them at the appropriate intervals. I was also lucky because Mr. Edgerton didn't really expect that much from the sophomores; he had more talented juniors and seniors who carried the tunes with flair and passion.

We knew better than to show up the upper classmen, anyway. Even the most talented of the sophomores knew that their turn as standout musicians would come later. We came to all the practices, learned all the routines.

I loved the grueling schedule of a Hillside High marching band member. It was no accident that Hillside had a great high school marching band. That hot summer we alternated on the football field with the football team and then, when school started, practiced before and after the school day. The adoration of our loyal fans whenever we played was worth the countless hours we sacrificed practicing.

While I enjoyed playing in the band, the thought of becoming a majorette was even more alluring. I watched them practice, and envied their creativity and talent. One of my best friends, Cynthia, a clarinet player, and I talked about how we were going to become majorettes. Cynthia got her older sister Roslyn to talk to one of the graduating seniors, Ava, who showed us the basics of baton-twirling and high stepping, and coached us on attitude and poise.

I loved it. We went to Ava's house as often as she had time for us, and then we went back to Cynthia's house for more work. We practiced and practiced. We both thought we had a good shot at being selected. We also knew that Mr. Edgerton had lost a lot of seniors on the twirling squad, and he was looking for talented sophomores. Somehow both Cynthia and I were selected along with four other sophomores, one junior, one senior, and our squad captain, Pam.

This was THE most exciting thing that I could imagine happening, and I proudly told all my family and friends. We were booked to play in the Mardi Gras, so Mr. E worked us hard. I didn't mind. I was a Hillside High School Marching Hornet and a majorette in the baddest band in the land, and we were going to New Orleans!

There were about a half dozen white students in the marching band my senior year. Allen, Tommy, and Andy vividly embraced the spirit of the band. They seemed comfortable in this setting—and excelled with this style of marching at Hillside compared to what bands were doing at the predominantly white high schools. No white girls ever tried out for the majorettes or flag squad—but the next year, Andy became the first white guy to lead the band as the drum major. Mr. E. rewarded talent, initiative and hard work. Andy had all three.

Out and About: Another Lesson Learned

I was a pretty good student, not the most outstanding because I had too many extracurricular interests, but I was regularly recognized for scholarly achievement. While this was a characteristic I was proud of, I sometimes wanted to shed my egghead reputation and adopt a hipper, cooler version of myself.

To avoid the embarrassment of having parents drop you off or pick you up at a party, my friends and I would tell our parents that the other's parents would take care of that. The objective was to arrive at the event or place via one of the desired ways: (1) boys, (2) a hitchhiked ride from someone we did or did not know (an older sibling was OK, but not someone's parent), or (3) on foot. Arriving at a party, park or dance accompanied by your parents was the worst possible situation, one to be avoided at all costs.

Many nights, I would get out of the house under some pretext of being picked up by one of my friends' parents. My friends and I would sit on the corner to catch a ride to a party or to visit boys in another neighborhood. Then we also had to find a way back home. Sometimes we caught rides with an older teen who already had his or her driver's license. He or she would drop us off at one house, and we would scatter back to our own homes in the vicinity.

This bad habit of hitchhiking around town was the highlight of our weekends. We looked forward to going out on the block (the corner of the street that separated our houses) to yell greetings at drivers we recognized. This became a game for us, mostly during the summer months, when we didn't have much to do. Then we started yelling at people we didn't know.

It was all good fun, and we passed many hours on Friday and Saturday nights, sitting on the corner, talking, calling at cars and chatting with whoever stopped. Sometimes we would coax the drivers to take us to the closest store if we wanted to buy candy, or to a house party. It seemed harmless enough, and we were always in a group, so we all felt safe.

One autumn day I was walking home from school after band practice. It was later than usual, and the friends I usually walked home with had already headed out, so I was alone. This was a comfortable walk for me, and I was lost in my thoughts about school, band practice and all that I had to do when I got home.

A car pulled up beside me as I climbed Lawson Avenue. I kept walking. The driver called out to me, "Hey!" I glanced in the direction of the voice and saw a familiar-looking face, although I could not remember his name or when I had met him. He asked if I wanted a ride.

I walked up to the car, and then I remembered. He was one of the guys we had stopped over the summer out on the block, so that made him OK in my mind. Besides he was kind of cute and didn't look threatening.

I hopped into his car.

At the next intersection he turned left. That was not the right way to go to my house, and I told him so. He suggest that I relax, that we were just going to do a little sightseeing, and besides, he needed to drop off a package at a friend's house. I could keep him company.

I tried to relax, to convince myself that I was OK, that this was OK. I started talking—about my friends, about school, about band practice, about my honor this and my honor that, hoping to impress him. He just kept nodding and driving, farther and farther away from my house.

We were on Roxboro Road when I finally realized that something was really wrong. He stopped talking. There was no longer a smile on his face. He just stared in front of him and accelerated. Suddenly, he swerved off Roxboro, barreling down an unpaved road.

I panicked and started screaming: "Where are you taking me? What are you doing?" He stopped the car suddenly and reached over me, locking my side of the car. I kept screaming. He pulled at my clothes—trying to kiss me, telling me to relax, that I knew this was what I wanted. I pleaded with him to stop, that this was all a mistake, that I was a virgin, that I was not that kind of girl, that I didn't even know him: "Stop! Stop! STOP!!" He tried to grab my breasts as I fought, and then I bit him. Finally, I was able to unlock the car and jump out.

I started to run toward the main road, crying, sobbing, crying, as I heard him crank up the car and pull up beside me. "Get in," he said, "I'll take you home."

"No way," I said to myself, no way am I getting back in that car, and continued walking. He rolled along beside me— laughing, and promising to take me home.

I thought a few minutes and reconsidered my options. How would I get home? I didn't have any money to make a phone call, I was too far away to walk home, and even if I could call my parents to come pick me up, what would I say? That was too humiliating.

I got back into his car.

He gave me a wry grin, knowing that I had no options. I hugged the passenger door, prepared to make another escape if I needed to. He ignored me, turned the volume up on the radio and drove me back to my side of town—to the street corner where we had first met weeks before, when I had been so confident flirting with my friends.

As I got out, he handed me my school books, and advised:

"Stop getting into cars with guys you don't know."

I still wonder whether his intention was to rape me, or just to scare me. I would like to believe the latter because nothing prevented him from accomplishing the first.

The rest of that school year passed comparatively uneventfully. I earned grades high enough to be chosen as class marshal for the Class of 1974. Although blacks outnumbered whites at Hillside, matters of academic achievement were always a balancing act, because only the students with the highest GPAs could represent the school for official events. Our dynamic and politically savvy principal, Mr. Lucas, was keenly aware that he was being watched by both the black and the white parents. Each and every decision had to be carefully weighed. One wrong step would bring unacceptable consequences. Frankly, I don't know how Mr. Lucas managed to walk that tightrope of racial angst, but he did. Decades later, he continues to receive accolades for his wise stewardship of our school during this period. Countless documents bear witness to his efforts.

There was always an equal number of black and white class marshals—always. That year, we also elected the first white class president at Hillside. Greg was an easygoing and popular guy—smart and funny—who had lots of friends both black and white. Greg's election seemed to demonstrate that our class had mastered this whole "integration thing."

The Second Letter

My senior year was on track to be the best of my life—I was in the band—and in May Mr. Edgerton told me that I was his choice to be head majorette! He said he wanted me to start working with the other girls that summer to make sure we were ready. Practice our twirling, practice our high stepping, make sure we were in shape, think about our uniforms, order our boots. I also had started dating a new guy, so things were looking good.

But then I got another letter.

In June 1974, the Durham City School Board sent a letter of correction notifying me I would need to change schools that year and that because of the zoning and where I lived, I needed to go to Durham High School. Their apologies.

My senior year—MY SENIOR YEAR!! How could they do this to me?! It was 1970 all over again. To say that I was horrified, grief-stricken, and could not be consoled does not convey the depths of my despair. I did not care that Durham High was a good school. I wanted to go to Hillside because I was a senior, I was the head majorette, I was a leader in other important school groups, all my friends were at Hillside, my boyfriend was there, and I just HAD to go to Hillside.

But the school board said "No."

I cried. I pleaded with my parents to do something, do anything, to help me stay at Hillside. Could we move? Could I move in with someone who lived in the Hillside area? Could I not move, but say we did and give a phony address? Plenty of kids wouldn't mind going to Durham High, so why were they torturing me? I had dedicated my whole life to stepping into my place at Hillside, and I was being denied...for what, FOR WHAT!?

I started telling all my friends that it looked as though I was not going to go to Hillside my senior year. Nobody could believe my bad luck. The idea of integration took on a terrible stench from my perspective. To me, integration was a hateful practice forcing people to go where they did not want to go for some unreasonable and arbitrary goal.

I knew that my parents were working behind the scenes, but I still do not know what tricks they pulled, what calls they made, what favors they promised, or what lines they crossed for me to stay in Hillside. I do know that I received another letter in June that I had been exempted from the new policy and could attend Hillside my final year.

The College Hunt

I applied to only a handful of colleges. The only one I was truly interested in was Spelman College, the historically black all female school in Atlanta. Spelman and Morehouse (the all male school also in Atlanta) were considered the best black colleges in the country. In early February, I was accepted and awarded a full four-year academic scholarship. All I needed to do was to send in the $100 housing deposit to guarantee my spot. I was thrilled. I informed my parents, and the $100 was sent. I started making plans to move to Atlanta.

Then I got an acceptance letter from Duke University, also with scholarship money, and my parents lost their minds.

"Duke!" they exclaimed to their friends. "Duke!! Our daughter got into Duke!" This was where my mother had toiled as an LPN for 30 years. She was in the first group of black nurses hired at Duke in the '50s. Black students were not admitted to Duke when my mother started working there. Nevertheless, from my parents' perspective, Duke was the Ivy League school of the South that guaranteed success for all who enrolled. Duke! Duke!

Many of my high school classmates, both black and white, had applied (and been admitted) to the University of North Carolina at Chapel Hill. I did not apply to Carolina or North Carolina Central University because I knew that I wanted to leave Durham. I applied to Duke, not thinking that I would be accepted, to appease my guidance counselor and my parents. So, when I received that acceptance notification packet on April 1 (yes, April Fool's Day), I was as surprised as anyone. I knew of Duke's reputation, and I was keenly aware that they admitted few black students. I had read that information in the newspaper.

When I saw my parents' joy and the amazement of all our family, friends, church members, neighbors, and Hillside teachers, it dawned on me that going to Duke was not about me or my accomplishments—it was about the success of the village that had raised me. I couldn't turn that down—no matter how much I wanted to go to Spelman. I acquiesced, put aside my plans, and sent back the acceptance note to Duke.

Graduation Season

I'd had a boyfriend for nine months, which, in teenager time, was a lifetime. As graduation approached, friends and others inquired if we were making long-term plans. I smiled and responded coyly—"Who knows?"—secretly hoping that it would be true. Our senior class peers had voted us "Best All Around" couple at Hillside. He was so smart, so athletic, so good looking, and we were so compatible in temperament, interests and ambitions. Or so I thought.

The end came quickly. He didn't have enough time, he said, and I heard my first (but not my last) "It's not you, it's me" routine. To his credit, he did take me to the senior prom a month later (though frankly I do not know whether it was from guilt, pity or familial pressures to help me save face so close to graduation). There were rumors of another girlfriend, and I was embarrassed and humiliated to have been dumped.

The acceptance letter from Duke jolted me back to life, thank God. The promise of a Duke education elevated my mood and poured salve over my wounded ego.

I graduated in June with a Hillside diploma, a list of academic honors and accolades, and a big family celebration. I was pleased with it all and settled in for a long and luxurious summer of doing nothing but reading Agatha Christie murder mysteries and hanging out with my friends. I figured I had plenty of time to think about fall classes and making the transition from high school to college.

But Duke had other plans for me that summer.

LaHoma Smith as head majorette at Hillside High School.
Courtesy of Hillside Hornet Yearbook, 1975

EIGHT
The Junior Miss Pageants

It was a priceless moment when we realized we had both represented Hillside in the Junior Miss pageant, albeit in different years. Though we had started talking about writing this book before that realization, finding that out might have sealed the deal for us both. We each wrote our own story about being in the pageant and shared them with each other afterward.

Cindy
What the World Needs Now Is Love: 1972

Junior Miss was a competition sponsored by the Jaycettes; high school senior girls were asked to participate in recognition of their grade point averages. With about a dozen other girls, I was called into a meeting in the early fall of 1972 by my high school counselor. After hearing the invitation, only two of us decided to take part—my friend, neighbor and future college roommate,

Judith, and me. Part of my motivation was the scholarship, and part of it was because the opportunity was flattering. I was proud of my academic achievements.

I was a bit worried about the talent portion; my artistic abilities were visual, not performance, and I thought it might be a stretch to use them in a competition. I also did not consider myself a beauty, but the Jaycettes stressed that this was not a beauty pageant—its purpose was to identify young women with achievement potential. As neither Judith nor I was involved in other extracurricular activities at school, this was a way for us to try to shine a bit and get some attention. Our mothers were both excited about this opportunity, and they pushed us to participate. I thought it might be a fair fight, though, by the end of it, I had changed my mind about a lot of things.

The Jaycette organization is the female counterpart to the Jaycees. The Jaycette ladies hosted an evening meeting at one of their homes for all 13 contestants so we could learn more about the pageant and what was expected of us. The Jaycettes were all proper Southern white ladies who did not work outside the home, used their husband's first names in reference to themselves (as was normal at the time—e.g., "Mrs. John Smith) and supported their husbands as they ascended in their professional careers. Jaycette sponsorship made this meeting newsworthy, and the event was the only occasion warranting my photograph in the newspaper while I was in high school.

Though the Jaycettes were higher on the social ladder than I was, I did not feel out of place in their homes. My mother was also a proper Southern lady, trained as a home economics teacher during a time when most people entertained formally. I was used to eating Sunday dinner on fine china, and I knew how to set a table and which fork to use when. I had no anxiety about eating the Jaycettes' dainty sandwiches with the crust cut off, served from silver trays, or drinking punch ladled from a crystal punch bowl. I knew how to behave.

The contestants—all of whom I liked—also spent time together at a local dance studio over the long Thanksgiving weekend before the pageant. We learned the two routines that were required—one for the physical fitness activity (a more modest substitute for the usual swimsuit competition) and one for the grace and poise activity—what was called the evening gown competition in the Miss America pageant. I quickly realized that the girls who were dancers had a huge advantage over the rest of us.

The physical fitness competition was a set of choreographed exercises, which we now call aerobic dancing. We wore double-knit stretch pants and matching long sleeve shirts that zipped up the front. We all wore different bright colors but with white belts and white tennis shoes. My outfit was tangerine orange. I shudder to think about it now.

I enjoyed the evening gown competition much more. It was a dance, but a slower one meant to show us off like belles of the ball, and the muted raspberry, velvet, empire-waist gown that my mother made for me was much more flattering than my fitness routine clothes. I loved that dress more than anything else about the pageant. We all wore satin pumps dyed to match our dresses and white gloves. I wore my long straight hair down and flowing. I felt as beautiful in that dress as I ever had.

We were told, honest to God, to put Vaseline on our teeth to help us smile. "You'll be so nervous; it'll be hard to smile. Your lips will quiver, and the Vaseline will make it easier," a Jaycette lady told us.

The preceding summer, I had been exposed to some similar "behind the scenes" beauty pageant communications. The Baptist youth conference I attended occurred in the same venue and simultaneously with rehearsals for the Miss South Carolina pageant. Contestants stayed on several floors above us in our dorm. We could hear the page on the intercom: "Miss Jones, please come to Room 222, and don't forget to bring your panty girdle," a disembodied man's voice crackled.

Also, we saw contestants at an outdoor cocktail party on campus, where everyone was in business dress except the young women competing for the Miss South Carolina title, who wore only bathing suits and high heels. In my newly awakening feminist world view, I had thought that attire was demeaning to those beautiful women. So when the pageant organizers told us about the Vaseline for our teeth, the suggestion didn't seem to me as demeaning as being publicly asked to bring your panty girdle to a rehearsal or standing nearly naked in high heels around fully dressed men. Not yet, anyway.

The weekend before the pageant, we were brought in one at a time for interviews with the judges at an afternoon reception. I wore an emerald green velveteen dress with long, cuffed sleeves, another of my mother's creations. And my white gloves. Three women and two men, one of them a minister, composed the judge's panel. The only question I remember being asked was, "If there were a man and a woman who were applying for the same job who were equally qualified, who would you give it to?" I thought it was a ridiculous question, and I do not remember what I said exactly. I must have given a somewhat ambivalent answer, because the follow-up was: "What if the man were married and supported a family, but the woman was not married or supporting a family?" I hesitated, but then gave them the answer it was apparent they wanted.

I have felt remorse ever since. I knew then the game was rigged. This whole competition was still part of the socialization of women to stay in their places, scholarship or not. My answer was not the appropriate feminist response, nor was being in the pageant the feminist thing to do. Though I felt resistance, I was not psychologically or emotionally equipped at that moment in my life to leave the interview or the pageant. I stayed, Vaseline teeth and all.

My "talent" was a dramatic reading. So was my friend Judith's. I recited a medley of 1 Corinthians 13 interspersed with lyrics from the song "What the World Needs Now Is Love (Sweet Love)" by Hal David and Burt Bacharach, made popular by Dionne Warwick in 1966. This New Testament chapter, I Corinthians 13, often read at weddings and referred to as the "love passage," begins, "If I speak with the eloquence of men and of angels, but have no love, my speech is no more than a noisy gong or a clanging bell." I wore a long dress of unbleached muslin with dolman sleeves. Mother made this one too, and I wore it often after the pageant. The reading expressed my Christian faith, and the dress was a bow to my hippie aspirations. Love seemed to me to be a safe topic. A piano version of "What the World Needs Now," played by the choir director from my church, accompanied my reading.

Contestant numbers were assigned in alphabetical order; as Cindy Stock, I was 13 of 13, so I was the last one to perform and waited nervously for my turn. I did well enough. I did not forget my lines. There was no hint of voice or drama training in my delivery, there having been none. "I did OK," I thought, but I knew it was not as impressive as a dance or music performance.

Judith, contestant No. 3, had recited John Donne's poem, "No Man Is an Island," with "Bridge Over Troubled Waters" in the background. We were both glad to have this part of the competition behind us. She had done a creditable job as well.

My father missed the pageant, which was a disappointment to me. My paternal grandmother, Augusta Stock, died several days before the event. She lived in Iowa, and I had not spent much time with her. She had sent me letters quite frequently and always on my birthday, with a dollar bill or two enclosed (which she called "leaves of lettuce"). There was no discussion of the whole family going to the funeral, pageant or not. My father went by himself, flying (a rare event) there and back over the weekend. Daddy usually took the family photographs, and because he was not at the pageant, I have no personal pictures from the event, only the newspaper photos, the program, and my contestant number to remind me of this transformative moment in my life.

The other bit of pageant-related drama was the appearance of my ex-boyfriend, Mitch. He started dating someone else almost immediately after he broke up with me that fall, and he brought her to the pageant! I saw him outside the auditorium when it was over. Though I was angry, I was polite in front of his new girlfriend, defaulting to my Southern lady training.

The Junior Miss pageant gave me some experience of the world and taught me a few things I might not have known otherwise. I met some girls from other schools and got a glimpse into the lives of the Jaycettes. It made me feel special—being invited, wearing pretty clothes. The discomfort I felt about the version of reality the pageant constructed about girls and women was a seed planted for later harvesting.

All the girls in the pageant that year were white. I have no idea of the racial composition of the girls invited to participate, but if there had been any black girls from Hillside or any other high schools, none of them chose to accept the invitation. I now wonder what barriers to their participation they felt. At that time, I was overwhelmed myself about the class and gender implications and never really got to a critique of the racial bias that resulted in all white participants, or all white Jaycettes for that matter.

Discussions today about race typically are focused on unconscious racial bias and white privilege—very different from the way we talked about race in the 1970s, which was almost all about stereotyping and civil rights. I did not think there were prohibitions about including black girls in the pageant. No black girls were there, though, and I did not question why.

LaHoma
You Gotta Have Somethin': 1974

I never missed watching the nationally televised Miss America beauty pageant. I loved watching the contestants parade out in their beautiful gowns, hairstyles, and perfect bodies. "There she is ...Miss America..." the white male host would sing "... Miss Alabama, Miss Alaska... Miss New York, Miss South Carolina..." With heads and busts held high in flawless fashion, all would walk onto the stage as the world watched "...There she is...your ideal..." the host crooned. The dreams of a million girls—I watched every second with envy and desire.

Sometimes my mother would pop her head in to ask: "How does Miss North Carolina look?" I would scan the girl in question and give my rapid assessment of her chances compared to the competition, never taking my eyes off the screen. If you could wish for one thing, Miss Kentucky, what would it be?... Batting long, curly eyelashes over those clear blue eyes, she did not skip a beat: "World peace," she would say (or something equally formulaic), and "save all the little children from hunger." "Nailed it," I thought, applauding my favorite.

I often wondered how those girls were discovered. Were they standing in line waiting for the bus or in a supermarket when someone walked up to them and declared they were the most beautiful girl in that city or state and sent them on their way to the national competition? Would the girls sit at home minding their own business, and someone would knock on their doors to inquire about the beautiful young ladies who lived there?

One thing was certain, though. In order to be noticed, you had to be white. Not that I expected the pageants to include girls of color, given that there were so few black women on television in general. So, even after watching the pageant every year, I never pictured myself entering a pageant of any kind.

I imagined that these women simply appeared, picked from obscurity to be placed on the world stage because of their amazing good looks, overflowing talents, and radiant smiles. So, when my high school guidance counselor asked me to consider entering the Durham Junior Miss Pageant, I was speechless. Me!? A pageant?!

Mr. Lawrence, a middle-age black man responsible for advising students on their college and career choices, convinced me that it was not a joke and was even a good way for me to earn scholarship money for college. Besides, the Junior Miss pageant was not a beauty pageant but rather a talent and academic achievement pageant. I had never thought about the pageants as a way to win money for college. I had paid attention only to the cars, jewelry, clothes, and modeling contracts that they featured for the winners.

As he showed me information about the Durham pageant, I wondered again if Mr. Lawrence was just teasing me, because only white girls were pictured on the flyers. But he told me that the pageant sponsors, the Jaycettes, wanted girls from Hillside to apply, girls like me, and he thought I would be a good representative.

Mr. Lawrence had submitted my name the previous year for an article on outstanding students in Durham. I had been the only black student featured on the cover of the newspaper. Because that had turned out all right for me, I trusted Mr. Lawrence and agreed to talk to my parents, even though I felt sure that the Jaycettes really meant that they only wanted the white students from Hillside.

I went home after school and talked it over with my parents.

Was there a cost? No.

Would I have to buy anything? Not really.

What would I have to do? Complete the application, participate in a number of promotional and educational events, get an evening gown to wear, practice a couple of dance numbers, participate in the pageant—and perform a talent.

What talent would you do? I don't know, maybe dancing, or playing the piano or twirling the baton.

And for sending in an application and participating in those activities, I might win scholarship money? Yes.

My parents, finally satisfied, said, "Yes."

I entered my name and received generally positive feedback from my parents, neighbors, and teachers. An article about the pageant appearing in the Durham Morning Herald, featuring me and a couple of the white contestants, helped to generate more interest and curiosity from my friends. Most of my friends were indifferent, since they believed, as I did, that a black girl didn't stand a chance of winning.

As I prepared for the competition in October, I wasn't nervous because I never believed I could win. I told myself that I was going through the motions to please my guidance counselor, Mr. Lawrence. It also felt as if this whole thing was yet another in a series of experiments in Durham. Given that this was the first year that the organization had actually recruited any black girls, we didn't expect much, and I think the adults were just glad to see more evidence of Durham's progress in bringing the races together.

The Jaycettes were always so polite; in fact, I had never met ladies that polite. Were they real? Perhaps I was just not used to being around middle-age white women, but I could not tell whether they were just being nice, as Southern ladies are inclined to be, or whether they were tolerating us for the sake of appearances.

I tried to imagine any of them getting angry or raising their voices to their children the way my mother and teachers often would display their dissatisfaction with us. It never happened. All the Jaycettes were kind and gentle, and they were probably just as uncomfortable as we were. Another step to racial unification in Durham. But all that didn't matter much to me, and I was immune to their genteel manners. I was used to outdoor camping and working in tobacco fields. My mother, my grandmother, my aunts, and the women in my neighborhood were real, and these women were not. But they were nice and polite, and they were helping me to be in a real-life pageant!

Each participant had a Jaycettes sponsor, whose job was to make sure that all of our needs were attended to for the pageant.

I think mine kind of felt sorry for me, since we all knew that I was going to lose. In fact, two of the 12 girls participating that year were black. The other black girl, Delores, attended one of the predominantly white county high schools. We never talked much. We didn't have time during our practices, and because we went to different high schools, we never connected beyond "hello" and "goodbye."

I think we were both surprised we were participating, but I never reached out to her, or she to me. My feeling was that I knew I was going to lose, and I didn't want to agonize too much about that. If Delores didn't know they'd never pick a black girl, I wasn't going to be the one to tell her.

Finally the big night arrived. My mother had bought me a new dress for the evening gown segment, and I felt really special. Because I knew I couldn't win, I did not feel the pressure that some of the other girls seemed to be experiencing. I had spent a lot of time preparing my individual talent performance— twirling my baton—so that I would not embarrass family, my Hillside or myself. My mother had made a spectacular outfit for the performance, and I was excited to be showing it off to the world. Because of my years in the band, I was accustomed to performing in front of large audiences.

The others girls were floating around, nervous, talkative, biting nails, twisting strands of hair— all in anticipation that they would be named Durham's Junior Miss. I was happy the day had arrived because it was the end to the crazy schedule of fitting these practices into my already hectic life as a senior at Hillside.

The competition was held at Durham High School—another sign that the evening would turn out exactly as I predicted. "Ladies and gentlemen," began the white male emcee, "Welcome to the 1974 annual Durham Junior Miss Pageant." We paraded out on the stage in our sports outfits to perform our first dance routine. I was confident and smiling. This was fun, and I was a good dancer.

"Next up, individual talent selections."

Nothin' from nothin' leaves nothin', sang Billy Preston. I twirled my body in my short sequined skirt, shook my hips in rhythm with the song…You gotta have somethin' if you want to be with me…and threw my baton high into the air and caught it.

Then we all paraded out in evening gowns to demonstrate our "ballroom finesse."

As the hour approached for the winner to be named, I got a strange feeling, and for the first time, I started to get a bit nervous. I had noticed the judges looking at me. I knew they would not bother doing that unless I was in contention. Could it be possible? Did I have a chance to win? At that moment, I started to care a little more as I imagined the impossible, that I might place, or that I might even win.

As the buildup to the announcement of the winners began, I looked around at the other girls and wondered whom my competition might be. I looked over at Delores. One thing was sure, if they picked one of us, the other one would not be selected. I was not very savvy in racial politics at that time, but I had figured out that the novelty of having black contestants would have its limits. So we waited.

Drum roll…

The announcer spoke…."Ladies and Gentleman, I am holding the list of winners. And the second runner up is… LaHoma Smith!"

Applause, applause, applause. I took my place in the winners' circle, beaming because I was right. They had been looking at me, and now I would be the first black girl to win a place in the Durham Junior Miss Pageant.

"And the first runner up is ...Susan Swindell..." Applause, applause, applause. Yes, Susan was a good choice. She would have been my first choice, with her beautiful brown eyes and long flowing hair. Susan and I had gotten along well in the pageant, even though she was a Durham High student. I was glad she was in the winners' circle, but now I was puzzled as to who would win. Whom had I overlooked? Who was more beautiful and talented than Susan?

We waited as the announcer again took the microphone. "And the winner of the Durham Junior Miss Pageant is... Delores Malloy!"

I am sure I gasped—along with the rest of the crowd. Then dead quiet as we all absorbed the announcement. Finally, the applause began and Delores came forward to be crowned. My emotions raced from puzzlement to pride to puzzlement in a matter of seconds. Another black girl won! Another black girl won! The first year they had included black girls in the competition, and we were awarded two of the three top prizes! Delores was a worthy, gracious, and lovely recipient... but I still couldn't get over it. The Durham community was spreading its wings, trying to show the world that it was becoming an inclusive place to live, work, and go to school. And I had to accept the first of many future unexpected outcomes based on skin color.

LaHoma Smith (far right) in the Durham Junior Miss Pageant.

NINE
From Black and White
to White and Black

Cindy

Such a relief to finally be leaving home and going to college! I was excited about my studies, but I was also excited about living my personal life. I was now able to make choices outside the strictures of my parents' watchful eyes, and what seemed like the arbitrary rules I had grown up with in my Southern Baptist faith.

My unfolding loss of faith meant the loss of a church community; this was scary but also a bit heady. I could not find reasons for prohibitions against drinking and sex (though drugs scared me), and I was ready to begin exploring my options. I still wanted to do well academically, though, so I proceeded cautiously, quickly discovering how complicated the notions of "right" and "wrong" can be.

The University of North Carolina (UNC) at Chapel Hill was a mere 15-minute drive from my parents' house in Durham, but I felt that I was in another new and different world.

* * *

At Hillside I had been a minority white face among a majority of black ones; this was not the case at UNC. Race was no longer a defining characteristic of my school environment, or at least that was my perspective as a white student at a predominantly white university. Within white spaces, which are most spaces in America, white privilege requires no recognition of our white selves as white, and race is not something we have to think about very much. At UNC I was back in my racial comfort zone.

My experience at Hillside had altered my view of the world. Those years had given me a different perspective about the black experience and an increased empathy for those affected by racial prejudice that I would not have had in a mostly white school. But, I was still white, and because I was white, I always had a choice of whether to engage in issues related to racial justice.

I had friends from Hillside at UNC—my neighbor and freshman roommate Judith and the boyfriend of one of our friends. We all lived in the older dorms on North Campus, close to most classes. Judith and I resided in the all-girls Cobb Dorm, an antebellum-style building with beautiful parlors on the first floor in which to entertain our beaus. Grand magnolia trees grew in our front yard and by the side doors, and, in Southern style, black maids kept the building clean for us. Only a few girls who lived in Cobb were not white. In the two years I lived there, I recognized the Old South plantation culture, and although I critiqued it, I was not sure what could be changed or how we might proceed to accomplish change.

I knew a few black Hillside alumni who were at UNC. I saw them infrequently; I had not been close to them in high school and did not get to know them much better in college. We talked when we saw each other in class or on campus but most of them lived on South Campus in the high-rise dorms, and there wasn't much mingling across the two sides of campus. I noted but didn't question too seriously why almost all the black students lived on South Campus, in another kind of segregation.

* * *

One memory illustrates how the racial figure and ground had changed for me in my new environment. One spring afternoon when I was walking across campus with a black student I knew from Hillside, I became aware that I was a white girl walking with a black girl. I wondered if other people noticed and what they thought. One moment, I had just been talking to a high school friend, and in the next moment, I was making a statement that I was the kind of white person who knows black people well enough to be having a conversation with them. Such interactions were not that common in 1974, even at my liberal university.

I was surprised that I had this thought. I was ashamed that I noticed and cared what other people thought. But I could not unthink it. I believed I was not supposed to "see race," but I was seeing it—even after my three years in a desegregated high school.

The Black Student Movement (BSM), a student organization at UNC, led the one protest on campus provoked by racial concerns that I remember from my college experience. The

Carolina Forum invited David Duke of Louisiana, the founder of the Knights of the Ku Klux Klan, to speak on campus; student fees paid for his trip. A dorm friend, Susan, and I were walking across campus the night he was there. We had not planned to go to his speech, but we were drawn to Memorial Hall when we heard loud chants of "Go to hell Duke" from more than 200 protestors. (This was usually heard at Carolina basketball games when we played the Duke University Blue Devils.) People were crowded in doorways and hanging out of windows to see the spectacle, and we soon realized that this protest was working—that there would be no speech by Mr. Duke that night.

The air around me was electric. I was not part of the protest, but I was there, elated and energized that others had kept David Duke from speaking. I understood the free speech argument for allowing him to speak, but I also felt there was great harm in letting him. I was literally on the outside looking in at this demonstration—in my comfort zone—sympathetic, moved even, but not in the middle of the action.

During my time at UNC, I never crossed over from concern and caring about racial issues to actual activism—I somehow was not able to pull myself out of my own life's requirements—now academic ones—to become fully involved. I was afraid of what activism would require and what I would have to give up. Activism looked appealing—the community, comradery, and feelings of purpose it must have created—but it looked overwhelming as well. I played it safe.

I took a course in race and politics in the South my second year, taught by a white professor who was an expert in Southern politics. He was liberal in his politics, which was comforting to me—I thought of myself as liberal also. I learned two new (to me) ideas from him. First, much of what was considered racism was actually classism, or at least it was complicated with classism. The second was that part of the reason there seemed to be less racism in the North was because fewer black people lived there and therefore white people had less reason to defend their territories.

Though I thought these were enlightening ideas at the time—and let my South off the hook a bit—now, decades later, I believe both that these ideas are untrue and that they obscured my (and everyone else's) understanding of structural, anti-black racism and the white supremacist culture in which we all participate. My professor was espousing a view that was considered progressive at the time, but the conversation about race was still about individual prejudice when I was taking his class.

I was particularly interested in his second point; I always had felt somewhat defensive about the South's reputation for racism vis-a-vis "The North." Of course, I knew Southern culture was racist and Southern white people had done awful things to black people for centuries, but I also believed they—we—were not more racist than people in the North. At least a strain of Southern liberalism had never condoned Jim Crow laws or any of the other unfair treatment based on race. I thought Northerners were not treating black people any better than Southerners were.

The citizens of Boston confirmed this for me when they were asked to desegregate their schools. I watched the protests against busing on television with my roommate Susan my senior year at UNC, thinking "those hypocrites." I felt some moral superiority because I had been part of a peaceful desegregation process in Durham, though I knew I had little to do with its "success."

* * *

The black people who were most visible in my daily life on campus were athletes. I was a big fan of UNC basketball, and though the team was not predominantly black, there were black first-string players such as Walter Davis and Phil Ford. (Michael Jordan joined the team shortly after I graduated.) For me, though, basketball players were beyond race. They were all minor gods. Race was less a part of their identity than their scoring average was.

There were no black coaches then. The exploitation of black athletes has been the subject of much discussion over the years: that few are prepared to compete academically, that academics are made easy for them to ensure that they play, and that many lack credible reading and math skills and often do not graduate. I would like to think this was not as true for the basketball players while I was in school as it is now, but I do not know. Carolina's famous basketball coach, Dean Smith, had been a civil rights activist in the 1960s, and I trusted that he treated all his athletes with respect and equity. It would be interesting to hear what the players then would say now.

One black former Hillside classmate was a walk-on on the junior varsity basketball team at UNC. Being a walk-on on the JV team did not elevate him to minor god status in my eyes, however. I had known him since seventh grade, and I knew he had gotten into UNC on his academic qualifications. We were both taking a jazz-appreciation class during our sophomore year. A real jazz trumpet player, not an academic, taught the class, keeping us alert with his beat-era slang and stories about his brushes with the jazz greats.

My former Hillside classmate, now UNC classmate/walk-on basketball player, had a reputation for dating only white girls (as did many of the black athletes). He started sitting beside me in class and hanging around to talk to me afterward. I was uncomfortable, not wanting to be just another white girl he went out with, so I kept my distance. In my mind I was not avoiding him because he was black, it was more that I did not want him to be interested in me because I was white. In retrospect, perhaps this assumption was unfair. Maybe I should have asked him what he thought.

* * *

Though worries about academic achievement had driven some of my concern about school desegregation, for me, those fears had proved generally unfounded. I had done well on the SATs and had gotten into a good state university. My college grades were providing further evidence. English composition, however, was the one subject in which, once I got to college, I thought Hillside had failed me academically. I had to work hard in many college courses, but no matter how hard I tried in my freshman English class, I just was not "getting" it. Something was out of my control, and I didn't know what it was.

We read such authors as Walker Percy and Gabriel Garcia Marquez. I loved their writing, and I am grateful to have been introduced to them in that course, but I could not write successfully about them. My writing assignments were coming back with massive amounts of red ink and terrible grades. I blamed my English teachers in high school for giving me A's but not teaching me how to write.

To be fair, I also blamed my uptight, red-lipsticked, chain-smoking (in class, stomping out the butts on the classroom floor!) graduate student instructor, for not reaching out to save me. I never considered going to her and asking for help. I was shy, and her unsmiling demeanor was intimidating. I hated her strangled laugh when she was being ironic and her visible irritation when students did not have the answers she wanted. I was mortified with the C I squeaked out of that class and continued to think for years afterward that I was doomed to poor writing skills. I believed these skills were unrecoverable, having missed learning them during a critical development period in high school.

* * *

There were few black faculty members at UNC when I was there. Within my discipline, psychology, I remember two, both assistant professors in clinical psychology. One of these was the only black professor I ever had at UNC as an undergraduate; I took a course in abnormal psychology from him. The other, a woman, not only eventually earned tenure; she also went on to become a dean. The university hired both of them about the time I started college, along with several other younger professors who exemplified more gender and racial diversity than the tenured staff. Very few members of this diverse cohort received tenure, however.

Race as related to mental wellbeing was not much studied in the psychology department at that time, although these two black faculty members did research on the effects of minority status. I was not uninterested in that. When I was in high school, I had read a lot of Robert Coles' work on the effects of segregation on black children in the South and was fascinated with his methods and findings. (Yes, I was truly a nerd in high school.) Feminist issues, such as sexism and the effects of women's changing roles, however, seemed more relevant to me while I was in college and during most of my research career.

* * *

Doing well academically was critical to my self-image, and a combination of fear of failure, introversion, and good study habits kept me psychologically centered during my years in school. Love and sex, however, were my other major preoccupations during college, my developing feminist ideology notwithstanding. Somehow I thought if I could just work out a relationship—had a boyfriend or a husband who agreed with my feminist ideals and principles—then I could redirect all the energy I spent worrying over not having a boyfriend toward my career. I would find out that this was fantasy—that none of us knew what experimenting with sex roles was going to mean. We didn't see that this would be a lifelong journey in which we would be making daily choices—not always the right ones—about how to integrate love, family, and career.

My dreams of romance were largely unfulfilled my first two years at UNC. There were boys I thought I was in love with, but these feelings were unrequited. And I had occasional dates with men I was not so interested in either. I still felt inclined to include sex in relationships even when my partner did not share my romantic feelings. I kept these experiences mostly to myself because the sexual revolution was not fully realized in 1973 in the South, and for most of my female friends, mutual love was still a requirement for sex. Luckily, I had one friend who lived in my dorm whose world view was more like mine; she became my confidante and, later, became my roommate when we moved out of the dorm. Thus, I did not feel completely alone in trying to figure out what was right and wrong for me in this confusing human realm.

My love life improved my senior year; I started dating the man I eventually married. He was the roommate of my roommate's boyfriend. He was a bit older, having been in the

Army until a few months before I met him. I thought he was beautiful. It was nice to have my feelings reciprocated, but there were a lot of ups and downs, and my hopes to have it all "settled" got a bit of a reality check.

As I tried to imagine life after college, the conflicts that women face about love and work, family and career were real for me. I felt caught in a tangle of how to use my brain and what to do with my heart. In principle, I never thought that I should give up a family to have a career or give up a career to have a family, but I did not know any woman who had had both in a satisfying way. I struggled with this dilemma.

* * *

The last semester of my senior year, my boyfriend quit school and moved to Raleigh for a job. Raleigh was not that far away, but I was insecure and worried that I might lose him from that distance. That year I was doing a senior honors thesis on women's sex-role conflicts. I was well aware of the irony of my anxiety about losing a romantic relationship while I was doing this research. Things worked out, though; my boyfriend and I got married the fall after I graduated.

My plan had been to go to graduate school in clinical psychology after I finished at UNC. That goal was partial motivation for going to summer school every year so that I could graduate in three years, thus reducing the total number of years I'd be in school before getting a real job. At the end of those three undergraduate years, though, I was feeling a little burned out, and I didn't want to have to make any decisions that might affect my budding romantic relationship, so I deferred going back for a doctorate. But I did graduate with honors.

Gender politics was what mattered in my day-to-day experiences, and gender politics was where I was putting my energy for social change. Gender shaped many choices I already had made and would continue to inform how I negotiated my way through family and career. I knew there was still racial prejudice in the world, and I knew it was wrong, but after three years in a white institution of higher learning, I still wasn't conscious of the unearned privilege that came with being white. It was just the air I breathed.

TEN

Discovering I Was Black

LaHoma

While Hillside had prepared me academically to be admitted to Duke University, once I got there, I realized that I was not prepared culturally. I migrated from a close and tightly knit Southern working-class black community in Durham to an unfamiliar Northeastern, upper-middle class and elite, mostly white community right across town. Although the distance in miles was few, the number of cultural miles traveled was immeasurable.

Hillside had instilled in me the confidence to think that I could excel anywhere—even at Duke—but my confidence quickly dissipated once I stepped onto campus. I had never visited the campus before I applied, relying, as most students had, on the academic reputation of the school as reason enough to want to attend.

I did not think much about race before I entered Duke in 1975, but I sure thought a lot about it when I graduated four years later. At Hillside, I had been part of the majority, the leadership, one of the smart kids, the honor kids, one of the students who had her pulse on everything going on in the school, who knew everybody, and was seen as a vital part of what made the school tick. At Duke, I was nobody. I did not fit in. I was not a leader. I was not seen as smart or sharp or vital to the school at all.

I quickly realized that I was not going to excel in this environment. The day after my high school graduation, I got a call from a black upperclassman at Duke who urged me to come to a boot camp to get to know the campus, take a few classes and meet other students. I didn't think I needed to attend the camp, especially because I had never had any academic challenges EVER in my life, and I made friends easily. The caller begged me to reconsider.

The only reason I eventually consented was because I did not have to make that great an effort to get there. I did resent the implication that I needed to do remedial work before beginning school in the fall. I was, however, not alone. About 40 or 50 students attended the eight-week residential summer program. All were black incoming freshmen. They were all smart, among the top 5 percent of their high-school classes, as I had been at Hillside. We all had been the leaders of our schools, and we all expected to do well at Duke.

We were told that we needed to make sure that we were able to keep up when regular classes started in the fall. This was a new experience for me. Never had I been made to feel that I might be lacking in academic preparation. A few of the upper-class black students were paid to serve as tutors for our English and calculus classes. The entering students came from all over the country—Atlanta, Boston, New York, and Washington, D.C. Krista became my freshman roommate. Val, Rita, Ronnie, Lil, Earlene, and Ernestine, among others, became close friends who helped keep me grounded through the most turbulent storms.

With these really smart black students, I developed a support system that helped me tolerate the sometimes hostile, mostly indifferent environment I was to experience at Duke. Some of those college friends are still friends today.

I started at Duke in the fall of 1975 with approximately 100 other black students from around the country—mostly the East Coast. By the end of that first year, half of them had left. They either dropped out or transferred to other schools. I knew many black students who, scarred from their early experiences at Duke, vowed never to return to that campus.

It was tough. I stayed primarily because a lot of black people from the Durham community, including my teachers from Hillside, believed in me. They were counting on me to finish to show the world that we could do the work. I met some wonderful people during my four years there, and I cherish a few of them as friends for life. But if I had it to do all over, I would NOT have gone to Duke.

I sat in classes with professors who insinuated through crude comments that black students did not belong at Duke. I was not used to being treated like a second-class citizen in the classroom, with subtle references and hints of discriminatory attitudes. I was not used to my intelligence being questioned and challenged. Probably one of the most puzzling grades I received at Duke was a C in Ebonics from a white professor. I guess I didn't demonstrate that I knew how to talk black enough for him. One semester, when I thought that I had been particularly mistreated, I decided to take matters into my own hands. I scheduled an appointment with the dean of students to complain about what I felt was an unjustified C in a course in which I thought (and my grades up until the final paper clearly supported) I deserved an A. I obviously delivered an unconvincing argument, because the dean seemed slightly amused by the entire conversation. How in the world did I dare to question the decision of the professor? I should be grateful to even be at Duke. Over the course of the past 40 years, I have forgiven those faculty members for making me feel inferior to the white students, but I will never, ever forget the pain of those memories.

Black instructors were few, and I had none my first year at Duke. I was fortunate to be taught by two during my other three years—one of them the legendary jazz pianist Mary Lou Williams, for whom the black cultural center on campus eventually was named. The other was a young sociology professor, who granted me permission to take his upper-level class even though I hadn't taken the prerequisite. I longed for some measure of validation from a faculty member. I did OK in his class, earning a B, but he made it clear that he had not signed on to be the "safe haven" for the black students, so he was not as available as I had hoped he would be.

Those of us who stayed survived through a combination of peer support and social support from the cafeteria and janitorial workers on campus, who let us know by winks and smiles, and extra large servings of food, that they were proud of us. My mother's cousin, Mr. Fieldpot, worked in the cafeteria, and I sought him out every now and then for encouragement.

"Never give up," he would say. "Never give up."

I did not share too much with him because I did not want to give the impression that I was not smart enough to stay, and I did not want him calling my parents to worry them. I was going to have to figure out pretty much on my own how to make this work.

My saving grace was the other black students on campus. We walked to class together, we lived together, we ate together in the cafeteria, we joined the same organizations, and we leaned on each other to help make sense of class lectures.

I rarely sought help from faculty members. I considered it to be a sign of weakness to ask for help from the white professors, teaching assistants or the white students, because doing so would just provide confirmation to them that we did not belong. So I refused to ask the whites on campus for help, seeking help in more unconventional places and people, such as my godfather, who was a math teacher at Hillside. He tutored me through my college math classes.

I knew almost no white students. Today, I am ashamed to say that although I remember a few faces, I can't remember more than a couple of white students' names from my days at Duke, while I remembered hundreds from my Hillside days. I did know white students who graduated with me from Hillside who also went to Duke, but we lost touch, and I did not see them at all during my four years. That's not to say that I didn't talk to white students; it's that none of them became people in whom I held any lasting interest or had any meaningful connections.

My black racial identity, however, grew stronger from one semester to the other. After a tenuous first year academically, I threw myself into organizations focused on improving the experience of black students on campus. I joined the Black

Student Association, the Black Dance group, and the Black Mass Choir.

As a member of the Black Student Association (BSA), I was responsible for bringing prominent black lecturers to campus. Ed Bradley of CBS and "60 Minutes" fame, the first black journalist to cover the White House, was one of the many famous personalities whose visits to Duke I coordinated.

We also protested the lack of black faculty, called for more cross-cultural studies and staged a sit-in of the Allen Building, the main administration building on campus. I respected the actions of the president of Duke, Terry Sanford, who met with us as we sat on the chairs and floor in the hallways and in his office. He told us he took our concerns seriously and that he would work with faculty and staff to respond to our needs.

I was initiated into a social group for one of the black fraternities, and I continued to surround myself with people and activities that seemed familiar from my Hillside days.

I did not avoid all white students and organizations. The end of my freshman year, the campus newspaper ran a notice of tryouts for the band's majorette squad. The only thing I knew about the band was that there appeared to be no black members. But I was curious and, given my experience at Whitted and Hillside, I ventured over to band practice to check things out. The similarities between Hillside's high-stepping Hornets and the Duke University Marching Band (DUMB) began and ended with the fact that everybody played instruments. The style of marching and the genre of music were completely different.

The band director, Mr. Henry, seemed genuinely pleased that I was interested in joining the band and encouraged me to apply for the majorette squad. Although the classroom had diminished my confidence in my academic abilities, I knew I could still twirl a baton. The chance to be a majorette in the band, to dance and create routines intrigued me, and I wondered—how bad could it be? So I tried out, with a fabulous (if I do say so myself) dance and twirl routine. Then I waited for Mr. Henry's decision.

I got the notice in the mail: "Congratulations! You have been selected as a majorette for the 1976 season…" I stared at the letter, surprised but pleased with the outcome. That was the most fun I had the next three years, going to all the home (and a few away) football games, although the band itself had a terrible reputation. My participation in the band was a source of constant teasing from many of my black classmates. I took it all in stride, because I agreed with many of their comments, and the joking was never done with malice or cruelty. I also felt that many of them were proud that I was breaking another barrier at Duke.

DUMB was not my Hillside marching Hornets, but it provided me with another type of lifeline to the Duke University community. By my senior year, another black student two years my junior, Tamra, had also joined, and our suggestions were regularly integrated into the squad's routine. That year, Mr. Henry selected me over two other girls to become the head majorette, featured at all the home Duke football games in 1978. My parents, being local, attended many of those games. Little kids (mostly white) would come up to me after the half-time show to get my autograph!

* * *

DUMB participation increased my visibility on campus, and I was invited to interview for the Duke Duchesses program. These young women were selected to serve as the official hostesses for important visitors and events at the school. I had never heard of the organization and had never seen an announcement inviting applicants, so when I told some friends that I planned to go to an interview, I could sense their disapproval.

"Why do you want to do that?" they asked me.

"Those girls will never accept you," they warned.

"You are just going to get your feelings hurt."

But someone also dared me to go—and I took her up on her wager. Had I not tried out for the majorette squad and succeeded?

So I applied, and I was accepted into a group I was never comfortable being around. I had neither the experience nor enough knowledge of etiquette to fit into the settings and receptions that entertained Duke VIPs. The next year, I did not bother to return. All the girls were cordial, but the effort to fit in did not seem worth it just to serve punch and cookies to Duke VIPs.

My racial lenses grew more discerning as the semesters passed. Sometimes this sensitivity caused friction even within the small black community of students on campus. Most challenging was the secret hostility that I felt toward black males, particularly black male athletes, who dated white females. During one particular week, marked by allegations of disloyalty to racial unity, we staged a "boycott" of the black males who were known to be dating white girls. The boycott strategy was simple: Don't talk to them; ignore them and disrespect them the way that they had disrespected us by choosing to date white girls rather than us.

There were two reasons for this reaction to interracial dating on campus. The first was the belief that, because there were so few black students on campus, we needed to stick together to survive. How could dating white people help us support one another? The other reason was more practical for us black females. Although the black males were successful in dating white girls on campus, white guys had demonstrated absolutely no interest in dating the black girls. Not one interracial couple was a white male and black female. Some of my black female classmates felt that the only dateable guys were the black guys, while the black guys had more choices and could cross racial lines. The boycott lasted only a couple of weeks, but it caused a lot of heated discussions among the black students, those who supported it and others who thought the boycott was stupid. Eventually things calmed down, but there were always whispers about the black male athletes, who seemed oblivious to any tensions, laughed them off, and continued to date whomever they wanted.

I can laugh now about how ironic it was that I participated in that boycott, because the love of my life, my husband of 30 years and the father of my children, is a white man. Given my loud opposition to mixed race relationships at that time, my 180-degree change in attitude is often met with a chuckle by those who attend our Duke class reunions. I also find it amusing that during one of the early reunions I attended, I ran into one of my former Hillside classmates, a white woman. When she introduced me to her spouse as a fellow Hillside and Duke alum, he looked me up and down and said "Hillside—you mean the ghetto school?" She seemed embarrassed, and I didn't know how to help her, so I made a quick exit. That is when I got my first inkling that my white peers had not shared my love of my high school.

Although many students came from high school or hometown traditions that celebrated homecoming events, Duke had given up the tradition of homecoming parades and royal courts, and there were no concerts featuring prominent artists to attract students, alumni, and area residents. Black students especially felt this lack, which was in stark contrast to the spectacular events surrounding homecoming at the historically black college across town, North Carolina Central University. A few black students tossed around ideas that led to plans to hold Duke's first-ever homecoming celebration specifically for black students. We were too few in number to have a parade, but we did host a number of activities, including a step show by the black fraternities and sororities, a banquet and a homecoming ball where we elected our own black homecoming court. Names of young women representing the four classes, plus another category for Ms. Black Duke, were placed on ballots. On the specified day, black students cast their ballots. The all-male committee collected the ballots and said the winners would be announced the following week at the homecoming dance.

I will not keep you in suspense. I won the Ms. Black Duke title. When my name was called, I came forward, wearing one of my mother's home-sewn dresses to take my place in the center of my court to the applause of our black classmates. I received a nice letter from the dean of minority students, and although there was no other real official recognition of this title by the school, I was satisfied. I had been accepted by my peers, and my identity as a black female at Duke had been affirmed.

* * *

There are many advantages to attending college in the town where you were raised. You can always eat a home-cooked meal and get your clothes washed, and, if you tire of dorm life, you can sleep in your own bed in your very own bedroom at home.

But for every advantage, there is a counteracting disadvantage. I tried to reconcile my high school life with my new college persona, and it did not always work. I also knew Durham better than most of my college classmates did, but I quickly realized that the Durham they saw was very different from the Durham I knew. Duke University was, and has always been, an anomaly within the Durham community. Duke created an enclave of mostly white, Northern, affluent students in proximity to a mostly working class and blue-collar town whose growth was fueled originally by the American Tobacco Company. The interdependency between students of money and privilege and working class folks who made the campus run was not always well understood by those students.

Each passing year accentuated the growing schism that existed between my life at Duke and the comfort and familiarity of home. In Durham and at home I felt smart, but when I returned to campus I was less sure of myself. By my junior year I was confident that I was going to be able to graduate from Duke, but I was still unable to escape the pull, tensions and limitations of my modest upbringing. I grew concerned that my natal world was too small.

The most concrete example of this emerging self-awareness appeared at the beginning of one of my required history classes—European history. I was often the only black student in any class. This class was no different—a fact of my life in a predominantly white institution. But the racial isolation had other disadvantages as well. I vividly remember the instructor starting the first day of class with the question: "How many of you have even been to Europe?" I looked around the room. Every student in the class raised his or her hand—except me. I was embarrassed. Was that a prerequisite for taking the class,

I wondered? Why was European travel a common experience for my classmates, yet it had never even come up in any conversations? I wasn't even sure where Europe was, let alone having traveled there.

I had little interest in learning from the professor or textbook after that. Once I saw that I was at a singular disadvantage from all my classmates who could easily conjure up images of France or Germany or England, I gave up on learning anything useful in that class. Their comments seemed insightful because they could visualize the sites. They spoke with authority because they understood the settings and context of places and historical landmarks and personalities.

Although this proved to be an agonizingly long semester, the experience began to sow a seed of desire in me to see the world with my own eyes. I wanted to become worldly and knowledgeable from direct experience, and not through the hand-me-down tales from books and TV shows that I had depended on for information. I knew I wanted to be the well-traveled person who could respond affirmatively to the question: "Have you ever been to Europe?" I eventually was. *Mais oui, j'ai bien réalisée ce rêve.* Yes, I achieved that dream.

Duke was also the chosen destination for many international students, including many South Africans fleeing the last vestiges of apartheid. I was especially attracted to two black South African students because I had only seen white South Africans on television. These two students defied everything I knew about South Africa and belied all that I had heard about the continent. They were always smartly dressed and articulate, using good grammar, and speaking English with British accents. I never heard them use any strange or native dialects. "Guma... guma...," as I heard on frequent episodes of Tarzan, was pretty much everything I knew about Africa other than news accounts about the current apartheid system. What was happening in South Africa in terms of racial oppression did not seem too far-fetched from what was happening to me, in Durham, in my opinion.

As we were walking together from class one day, I remarked, this time, aloud to the South Africans, how well they spoke English, and I wondered how long it had taken them to learn it. They looked at each other, thanked me and muttered something about how all South Africans speak English. The irony in their voices did not make much of an impression on me at the time, and it did not keep me from making a fool of myself.

"How do you get information from home about what's going on in your village?" I asked. "How do the mail carriers get from tree to tree to deliver your letters? Aren't you scared of the lions?" They looked at each other again, and this time, they did not hide their disgust.

"May I ask you a question?" one of the young men responded. "Are all Afro-Americans as ignorant about Africa as you are? We don't live in trees!" They both walked away, leaving me bewildered about what I had done wrong.

My quest for knowledge about Africa began at that moment, when I realized that I had been lied to all those years, and that I did not know that I had been lied to. And I resolved to leave Durham to find out for myself. I was no longer content to just be a Duke student (or soon, a Duke alum). I had led too circumscribed an existence, and I could not even claim that I had left home to go to college. At least most of my high school classmates had done that.

It would be foolish to attribute my career path to any one factor or institution. I feel blessed to have had experiences and people who believed in me from College View Nursery to Whitted, then Hillside, Duke, and the University of North Carolina.

My determination to stick it out at Duke can be credited to a supportive community in Southeast Durham. I survived and graduated in four years because of their love and from sheer force of will. I persisted because I knew I would be the first in my family to graduate from college. I knew that a lot of people were counting on me to do well. I could not bear to disappoint them, and I couldn't think about anything other than proving that I really did deserve to be at this university. I believed that I had earned my admission ticket, and I managed to tread water when the sharks were circling and the expectation was that we black students would all drown at sea.

I didn't talk to my parents much about my challenges at Duke because I didn't want to worry them. They also did not know about internships and networking with alumni and the benefits of pledging one of the sororities. And because they hadn't gone to college, they couldn't tell me that I should pursue those opportunities, so I didn't. I hoped that completing the degree would be good enough.

ELEVEN

Taking It With Us

Our discussions about this book always began with conversations about every other part of our lives besides the memoir—our children, our spouses, our parents, friends, politics, work, play, all of it. This is a memoir about race, but we also reflect upon our personal lives, our lives today, because as we wrote about our school experience, it was impossible not to think—together and individually—about what has happened since our school days and continues to happen. We found ourselves thinking about what all of this calls us to do and how to act on our concerns.

Cindy

When we first realized that we had both gone to Hillside and started talking about our experiences there—before we even thought about writing this book—I think I said something to the effect that being at Hillside had had a big influence on my life. I might have even stated that I was grateful for this experience because I had learned so much that I might not have learned any other way. When I heard from LaHoma that she had not exactly been a big fan of integration at Hillside, I was fascinated. And these stories that we told each other became our book. Having gone through the process of writing this book—really going back in my mind to remember specific people and incidents I had not thought of in years, remembering them in the context of all of my life that followed—I still agree with my initial, if somewhat (at the time) blithe answer, but I now am grateful for reasons that are more concrete and nuanced.

I carried a story about Hillside in my head for many years, bringing it out only occasionally when it seemed relevant or when I needed some race "cred." The events that led to writing this book, and even more the writing of this book itself, however, have given me the opportunity to revisit the story I was holding on to, to re-remember, question some assumptions, and see how I may have reconstructed some of it to fit with a simpler life narrative. It is in understanding these inconsistencies that I have gained the most useful knowledge about myself as a white person who wants a better way for America when it comes to racial equity and justice. Stripping back some of the varnish—owning up to my past and present biases—has helped me see myself as a "work in progress."

Going to high school at Hillside physically situated me in a black space for most of my day for most of the week for most of the year for three years. What I learned there that I carried with me into further schooling, my career, political involvement, volunteer work, marriage, and childrearing was what it was like to be a minority (though not an oppressed one) in another culture (albeit not a completely foreign one). I was more inside another kind of life than I would have been otherwise, and it was not harmful to me, and in fact, there was much to celebrate about it and to feel affection for. I learned a certain kind of ease in being with others who, outside of Hillside, would have been a minority in my usual space. I learned to feel comfortable across "difference."

I have no illusions that I had the "inside out" version of black students sent to predominantly white schools. I was never expected to assimilate, and black students would have thought it odd if I had tried. We white folks were visiting and were expected to be as polite as our hosts were being to us. Southern rules of etiquette apply to all races. Even if there had been a continuing white presence at Hillside beyond the few years it occurred, no one would have expected assimilation ever, just a greater understanding between us and greater acceptance and tolerance for the differences in our lives.

I have no doubt that being at Hillside meant I had greater exposure to issues of concern and interest to black people than if I had been at the predominantly white Durham High School. I studied black literature and art at Hillside, and this was consciousness-raising for me. I heard more black music and liked it more than I would have otherwise. I sometimes saw how Hillside was treated differently (with less respect) because it was a predominantly black school, despite our relatively small white presence. All of these things stayed with me, inside of me somewhere as I went on with my life.

An "ah-ha!" moment for me in writing this memoir was realizing how much my world, while I was in high school, was still a very white world outside of Hillside. Though I shared physical space with black people during the school day, so many barriers still existed between us. During high school, most of my life was still in a very white world. LaHoma and I walked the same halls for a whole school year—and I might have recognized her then as a fellow student—but our lives were lived very separately. Then, when I left Hillside for college, I was solidly back in a white world.

And though I had concern and sympathies and perhaps I even thought I understood something about racial prejudice, I did not rush headlong into trying to fix it because of my experience at Hillside. Awareness of racial prejudice was tangential to many of my academic and career interests, but never front and center—at least not initially. I was all about righting wrongs, but I was more focused on sexism and the rights of women and girls (of all races).

That interest in women's causes led me to do volunteer work with more than one organization as a reproductive health counselor. After I did coursework for my master's degree, that interest led me to apply for a job as a research assistant in international family-planning research. After six years, I returned to graduate school so I could refocus my interests on the social and behavioral aspects of reproductive health. I specifically focused on adolescents, remembering both the amazing (in retrospect) information I got in 10th grade biology class and the girls at my library table from my world history class who already were mothers. I could not put those two things together. Now I can—but that lack of understanding on my part led me down a career path that had me thinking a lot about the role of race and poverty in women's lives. After my coursework for my doctoral degree, I took a job at a public-interest organization whose mission was the reduction of teenage pregnancies. Most of its work was domestic, and the research I did there opened up my consciousness in many ways, but I think I had been primed for these insights by my experiences in high school.

One way having been at Hillside influenced my personal life—which for me was very intertwined with my work life— was that I had a level of comfort with being in black spaces and with black people, and I developed an interest in black culture. I believe it made me more receptive to listening to what my adult friends who were black were telling me about the way racism operates in their lives. For example, a black colleague told me that during a work meeting where we both were present and talking, another white person in the room looked only at me when she was talking. I had missed this non-verbal transgression, but the observation sensitized me to see it in many subsequent cross-racial work interactions and to be mindful about not doing it myself.

My first husband and I consciously tried to raise our children to value everyone and be inclusive in their relationships. It was hard for them to understand what had gone on before; when we watched *Eyes on the Prize* on PBS with our daughter, then in elementary school, at one point she turned around to us and said, "This didn't really happen, did it?" She could not believe that policemen would turn hoses on peaceful protestors, black or white. We neither encouraged nor discouraged friendships on the basis of race or wealth (we were firmly in the middle of the economic spectrum in our highly resourced community). We spoke out about big and small injustices when we saw them and encouraged our children to do the same. But the main thing we did was teach them that the Golden Rule applies to everyone. Neither of them ever questioned this belief or behaved in a way that made us doubt their commitment to equity.

Another part of the answer to how being at Hillside influenced my life is revealed by more recent events. Fast-forward to about eight years ago. I had begun thinking about what else I might want to do with my life, things that I had not been able to do in my job. Throughout my life, I had been interested in writing. My job required very academic writing, restricting some of the more soulful and passionate ideas I wanted to share. I started taking creative nonfiction writing classes and workshops. At the same time, I saw how racism was still afflicting people around me. Perhaps I had just reached a tipping point after an accumulation of experiences and years of thinking about the issue. I felt a calling to do something, anything.

I became aware of a theology that provided a framework for community and action around the issue of racism, under the broader banner of "peacework," a concept central to what my spiritual faith meant to my life. If faith was not about compassion for everyone, what was I missing? I was inspired by a talk by author Tim Tyson to join the NAACP. Rev. William Barber II, a North Carolina and national NAACP leader, inspired me to join in Moral Monday marches at the General Assembly building in Raleigh to protest the dismantling by Republican-led state legislators of every kind of political protection and social safety net for North Carolina's most vulnerable citizens. My participation in a two-day anti-racism workshop conducted by the Racial Equity Institute of Greensboro, N.C., turned my thinking upside down as I saw the truth of America as a white supremacist country. I grew more aware of unconscious racial bias and began to see my white privilege in action. I thought I had known something about the effects of prejudice, but I came to understand through this multiracial workshop the greater power in understanding structural racism and the need to dismantle systemic racism, so that black lives truly matter.

As I was preparing to leave a career of nearly 30 years as a reproductive health researcher, I was also preparing myself for a fuller commitment to activism for racial justice. I joined our town's Justice in Action Committee and learned about the school-to-prison pipeline, the difficulties in transitioning from incarceration to "normal" life, and the many challenges of finding affordable housing in my town. There are many avenues for working toward racial justice, because the effects of policies to maintain the advantages of being white seep into every aspect of life one can imagine.

My experiences at Hillside planted a seed and prepared the soil. Schools cannot, in one year or 12 years, upend centuries of institutionalized racism and unconscious racial bias. But what being at Hillside did was open my consciousness to the possibility that the world is different for different people, and that race most certainly creates different opportunities and barriers for people who might have the same set of abilities. My time there gave me a certain comfort level with people who were different from me. It allowed me to be in those spaces, to hear the conversations and, most of all, to believe what people tell me about how their experience is different from mine. There is probably no straight line between my having been at Hillside and a particular thing I say or do now, but that experience has led me through a series of other experiences that have made me feel the urgency for anti-racism activism at this moment. There was not an instantaneous moment in which my (conscious or unconscious) racial bias was eradicated, a moment when I became a perfect conduit for dismantling racism. I am still not without this bias. But my consciousness did change, even if it changed in some ways that might not have been translated into action until later in my life. My experiences at Hillside led to or connected to other experiences. Change of consciousness is a slow-building process—an iterative process—with each new idea or action building on previous new ideas and experiences.

Writing this book with LaHoma is part of this journey for me. It is important that we have written it together. Hearing each other's stories opened us up to remembering stories we had forgotten, or to see our own stories in a new light. Bringing together our separate narratives illustrated the need for our differing perspectives to be told side by side, as a way of generating discussion to heal the harms inflicted by racism.

LaHoma

Years ago, if you had asked me whether "the letter" and grade school integration had been a positive influence in my life, I would have responded with a resounding "Yes!" Over the course of writing this book and as memories surfaced, I started to have my doubts. Now that we have come to the end of our project together, the doubts have largely subsided, but my initial enthusiasm is far more circumspect, my answer less confident and more likely to be qualified by "Well, it depends."

I have mused incessantly over whether there are indeed benefits to forced school integration of black and white communities. I found blogs of white students who hated Hillside and cursed their days at the school. Of course I am sympathetic, because when I was going through that social experiment myself, I resented it as well, but not because I hated the white students; I just didn't see the point of making us go to school together. My attitudes have softened, and now I find myself somewhere in the middle of this discourse. I can easily champion a defense of either side. Let me explain.

For the affirmative, I embrace the notion that attending junior high and high schools with students from different racial groups gave those of us coming from segregated communities the chance to interact with white students on a level playing field. Yes we could go into a store and see a white person, we could go to the movies and we saw white people all over television, but in school we were equal, we were classmates and we were friends who interacted with each other based on similar interests, from the band to the French club.

But one could ask, "Beyond sitting beside someone of a different race, was anything of substance gained from those interactions?" Many of those relationships were superficial and limited in scope and intensity. We greeted one another with a casual "Hey, how're you doing?", but beyond that, it was rare to see close connections between black students and white students. Yes, a few boys, mostly the black male athletes, developed more intimate relationships with the white female students, usually also athletes. But any interaction outside of school hours would have been unusual for most of us. I certainly never brought anybody home with me. I do remember occasionally visiting the home of one of my white classmates, Helen, who had also been a contestant in the Junior Miss pageant. She was also one of the smartest students at Hillside, and we had a lot of similar interests. Our relationship was warm and cordial, but more important, it allowed me to see her as a human being, as just another girl, even though she was white.

Was that relationship, or similar ones, unworthy of obtaining simply because it did not result in lifelong friendships? Is the mere interaction too superficial an outcome? As a first step for people who have very little contact with each other outside of school, why wasn't just bringing people together for the betterment of our society a good enough goal?

As I promote this argument, I can see other benefits. Integration permitted us to satisfy our curiosities about the other group, develop new attitudes, and challenge stereotypes about people within the context of a safe environment. I was surprised, for example, to learn that not all white people were high academic achievers. Up to that point, I had been convinced that all white people in the world were really smart, all the beautiful people were white, and all the best things in life belonged to white people. To me, that belief was more a fact than a complaint.

When we got to Hillside, I saw another side: that not all white people were in the Honor Society, and that black students could excel in activities even when white students were involved. White students also saw black people and realized that their perceptions and stereotypes about blacks were flawed. Not all black people are poor or can dance and sing.

Recently, I scanned my high school yearbook and noticed a picture of one of my black classmates braiding the long, blond hair of one of my white classmates. Little did they know that they were well ahead of Bo Derek's trendsetting cornrows in the late 1970s. These benign interactions, on the surface harmless and pointless, permitted unspoken questions, each about the other, to be answered: "What does your hair feel like? Why does it stay so straight? My hair is curly." Innocent curiosity led to interactions and explorations in a safe space. Cindy's annoyance at the formality and social traditions at Hillside helped her achieve proficiency in cross-cultural settings and more easily adjust as a working professional in settings with people unlike herself.

A prevailing sentiment among black students was that, even though we recognized our differences from the white students, we acknowledged that the white students who attended Hillside were the "good guys" because they had chosen to be with black students, while the white students who did not want to be there did not come. We believed that our white classmates had parents who weren't scared of their children mixing with us. Cindy's high school stories reveal that those impressions were not entirely accurate.

That is not to say that white students always felt welcomed or well assimilated into Hillside's predominantly black culture, but neither were they shunned. There weren't riots or racial fights. The black students tried to display their understanding that the white students had good intentions. So, for the most part, there was no need to intimidate or create a hostile environment, because these white kids were the ones who decided to stay. They were harmless and benign, and they were there because they and their families had decided for whatever reason that it would be OK to be at Hillside. As for the people who were not at Hillside, those who were being transferred off to Durham Academy or wherever? We did not encounter those people. It was the people who made the decision to be there who were there. So there was a friendly atmosphere, and we got along, and for the most part we did not go beyond that. At least I did not.

When I realized that Cindy had attended Hillside, I gained renewed respect for her. We had a shared past, if not a shared perspective about our experience. Of course, now I realize that there might have been white kids who didn't want to be at

Hillside but who had no other options or resources. Not all the white students' parents were liberal professors at Duke. At the time, we did not make those distinctions among the white kids, assuming that everyone was there by choice.

While we generally accepted our white classmates, we were not deaf to the strong opposition to integration we heard from outside our walls. We heard about it from our parents, read about it in the newspapers, and listened to discussions on the radio and television. We mainly felt insulated from those discussions. Besides, in Mr. Lucas' high school, we were not going to be permitted to participate in any funny business.

Mr. Lucas' leadership through this period in Durham cannot be overstated. While working as our principal, he was also a leader in discussions to achieve racial integration at all levels of the educational system in North Carolina. Hillside was seen as a model of what was possible, and Mr. Lucas was a frequent spokesperson for the merits of bringing black and white children together. His interest, he said, "is to seek a strong voice for education with equal opportunity. My concept was that in order to merge, you should bring two groups together on an equal footing." (9) Since his retirement, Dr. Lucas has continued to lend his voice to advocacy for educational issues in a number of capacities at the local, state, national and international levels.

To counter these arguments, I could also defend the narrative that people should be allowed to attend whatever school they want to attend—even if that choice means that they want to be among the majority race in that school. My attitude is a reflection of where I currently sit. After attending Hillside and then two predominantly white universities, I am now a professor at a historically black university, North Carolina Central University in Durham. NCCU is composed of a predominantly black student population, oriented toward traditions, culture, and a legacy of social justice and service to the black community. NCCU is also one of 16 campuses that make up the University of North Carolina system. Of the 16 campuses, six are HBCUs (historically black colleges and universities). The demographic trends of the university are changing, and I suspect that the increase of enrollments from white, Latino and Asian students will provide for even greater diversity on campus. But the culture of the campus is likely to remain strongly rooted in its commitment to educating the black community.

The reason there are six HBCUs had nothing to do with choice, but rather that other state-funded schools did not allow for the admission of black students until about 50 years ago. To quell discontent, the state legislators began to provide some financial support to these black schools and eventually brought them into the UNC system.

I continue to be annoyed by the obvious differences in resources between the HBCUs compared to the larger institutions—all supposedly equal members within the UNC system. What is the rationale for the disparities between the campuses and the differences in perceptions in the quality of the academic experience? Being a Durham girl, I knew that there were differences in perceptions, but it was only after I started working at NCCU, after many years of working in international development, that I learned that those differences in perception were a result of actual differences in how resources were allocated, how decisions were made and how faculty and staff were affected in terms of research, teaching and service activities. As the years have progressed, I have grown increasingly resentful, and now I'm pretty defensive about the whole situation.

Today, black students are not limited at all by their choices or their ability to attend majority institutions. Many choose HBCUs even when they have many, many options and would be successful regardless of their university setting. I have come to realize that some students benefit from the nurturing environment that campuses like ours offer to black students. Perhaps the nurturing environment of Hillside paved the way for my success. So who cannot argue that the selections of schools should really be the choice of the students and their families? What is so magical about this experience at a predominantly black college that parents might not also make this choice if it were allowed at elementary, middle, and high schools? Certainly there are those currently pushing this agenda as a viable path for black children.

Some data suggest that black children who attend integrated schools are more likely to succeed, score significantly higher on standardized math tests and enjoy higher earnings and rates of employment later in life. Studies report that black students who attend schools with whites are less likely to bear children as teenagers, or to be incarcerated as adults (10). Other studies cite the positive influences of same-race role models in the classroom, particularly for black males, and the importance of learning in an environment that is not perceived as racist and hostile (11). Who is right?

The truth, I believe, lies somewhere in between. I believe that school integration is an important component of living in a multiracial society. We cannot claim to value equality while holding on to policies that make it easy to maintain separate instructional facilities based on skin color. Court-ordered desegregation efforts that compelled children like Cindy and me, comfortable in our own respective worlds, to move out of our safe cocoons to explore the worlds of others were important. We developed flexibility and skills to move easily in and out of different cultural settings. We learned how to negotiate and survive challenging situations and bring up difficult topics about race in nonthreatening environments. While some would argue that meaningful dialogue at Hillside was limited, learning to live and work alongside one another served an invaluable purpose. It led me to want more for myself, to do more for my community and to accept that there were white people just like me, with similar interests and values. I am sure that it did the same for Cindy. Some of those lessons were learned at Hillside; others I learned at Duke and beyond.

Creative and innovative approaches that offer dignity, respect, equality, and recognize the value of each and every student, regardless of race, are still needed. However, we should not pretend that current efforts to return to neighborhood schools and give parents the choice of taxpayer-funded charter schools are anything more than a desire to move away from school integration. As a nation, we are slowly pulling away the foundation from a hard-fought legacy worthy of holding on to. We seem willing to toss aside the bricks of time, effort and understanding that were so carefully crafted by Dr. Lucas and the pioneers of the desegregation movement. We are returning to silos of convenience and comfort, and though we pretend to respect integration, we are moving rapidly ahead to support school board members and policymakers who will ensure that integration is never fully achieved. The experiences that Cindy and I contemplate provide greater context and justification for fighting for school desegregation, even as our nation charges full steam ahead to destroy it.

TWELVE

Sending Our Kids to School

When the courts ordered schools to desegregate in the 1970s, white parents (and some black parents as well) made decisions about whether to comply, or to resist by moving out of the school district or sending their children to private schools. One topic we talked about as we were thinking about how our school desegregation experiences influenced us was the role race played in decisions we made as parents about our own children's schooling.

Cindy

My children both went to school in the Chapel Hill-Carrboro City School district from kindergarten through graduation from high school, except for a two-year break when my daughter was in fifth and sixth grades while we were living in Fairfax County in Virginia, and I was working in Washington, D.C. I went to college in Chapel Hill, and I always loved it there.

I loved it as a small town and as a university town. My husband and I were living in Chapel Hill when my oldest, Emily, was born, having moved there after a year in Raleigh and almost two years in Flagstaff, Arizona, where I got a master's degree. When my daughter was born, my husband was planning to go back to school in Chapel Hill to finish his degree and get a teaching certificate. We were great believers in the public school system—whatever that meant to us at the time—for socializing our kids.

We could have moved to Durham. Having grown up there, I was comfortable there; my parents were still living there, and it was cheaper. But we chose to live in Chapel Hill instead. We liked being close to the university, the city was smaller, and we had friends there. And we also knew that the school system there had better resources and a better reputation for academic achievement. We were willing to pay more in taxes and live in a smaller house. Eventually, John taught school there.

Chapel Hill's school system was much whiter than Durham's, which at that time was working through a merger of the city and county school systems. Not only were Chapel Hill schools whiter, but also there was a lot of wealth privilege among its students. We did worry about our children getting a skewed view of the world because of that affluence. Our kids had us as parents, though, so there was always discussion about what was going on related to racism and civil rights. We did not see school as the only means of socialization in regard to race. We felt that being in school in Chapel Hill versus Durham (or anywhere else) was not going to be detrimental to their beliefs in racial equity. They were still in classes with black children, and they had black teachers. Both had black friends at school with whom they socialized in and out of school. My daughter had a great elementary school experience, and so did my son. And they were close to home.

As a parent and someone interested in racial justice— and given my own school experience—I sometimes consider whether I should have made other choices. Would being in a less white, less wealthy school system have been better for my children? Given them a different outlook on the world? In the end, I believe the proof is in the way they grew up. They are both very conscious of racial justice issues. My daughter is active in anti-racist advocacy wherever she is—now in Ireland. My son is not an activist, but he steps up and speaks out when necessary.

When I was in high school, I was judgmental about the families that sent their kids to private schools, because I believed it was important that people try to make desegregation work. I did not know exactly how desegregation was going to change things, and my racial consciousness was not sophisticated, but I just thought if this was something important to do, why doesn't everybody play by the same rules? But then as you become a parent, and you weigh decisions about the welfare of your children against the greater good, sometimes decisions are not so clear-cut. It is very easy to be inconsistent when it gets personal. It is a moral dilemma that I struggled with. I think it is important to be honest about that, even if doing so complicates my self-image.

During the time we have been writing this book, I became a grandmother, and I have been thinking about what kinds of decisions my son and daughter-in-law will make for my granddaughter's education. I hope that my granddaughter will be living in a community where there is racial and class diversity and she can go to a nearby public school that reflects that diversity and where her parents feel comfortable with the quality of the education she will get.

LaHoma

I did not really think about school for my children until I had to make a decision about daycare. When we bought our house, we were both just starting new jobs. Although we knew that we wanted children, we did not have kids, and I did not even think about looking around at schools. We were so focused on the affordability of the house. I guess I just assumed that the school system would be good. The one thing that I regret about our decision to live where we eventually did is that it limited our public school choices. When our children came along and we started to explore the local school system, I was less than pleased with what I found. It wasn't bad, but it wasn't what I was expecting, either.

My husband, Tim, had been a graduate student and then a stay-at-home dad when we first became parents, while I worked and we lived in Washington, D.C. When we returned to our house in North Carolina, and Tim found a job, we knew we needed to find care for our soon-to-be 3-year-old baby girl.

My parents, both retired by then, agreed to look after her until we found a more permanent arrangement, so I began the arduous and meticulous search for the best care we could afford. Of course it made sense to look in our small rural community even if we were not very familiar with it. My preference was to find a home arrangement with someone who had only one other child, so I asked around my family. Eventually, by word of mouth, I visited half a dozen home-care facilities in the area. None of them met our needs.

After a couple of weeks of these futile efforts, I knew I needed to expand my criteria, so I reached out to a local church that I passed every day on the way to work. I had noticed small children playing in the backyard of the church grounds, and because the church was so close to my house, I thought that this arrangement would be wonderfully convenient. One day, once I arrived at work, I looked up the number in the phone book and gave them a call. The lady who answered the phone was "delighted" that I called. She said of course they had openings, and they would love to show me the facility at my convenience. I told her that the daycare was close to my home and asked her if anyone would be there to show it to me on my way home that very evening. She assured me that they would still be around because they did not close until 6 p.m. She would be waiting to give me a tour and answer all my questions.

I hung up the phone relieved that she had been so accommodating and that it looked as if I had finally found a place for our daughter. I left work a few minutes early and drove the 40-minute commute from work to the church daycare. I walked up to the door and rang the bell. A middle-age white woman opened the door, gave me the once over and asked, "Yes, may I help you?" with a rather icy tone. "Yes, hello," I replied, alarm bells softly tinkling in my head, but not wanting to overreact.

I continued, "I am the lady who called earlier today to ask if there were any openings. I spoke with someone who said that I could stop by this evening to get more information and go on a tour of the facility."

The woman did not move from the doorway. "Well, I don't know who you talked to, but we don't have any openings here."

She offered nothing further. I could not believe what she was saying.

"Are you sure?" I replied, my voice shaking. "The lady with whom I spoke sounded as though you had lots of openings, and that is why she invited me to stop by today."

"No, sorry, she must have made a mistake."

By this time, I realized what I was dealing with, but I wanted to see the performance through to its logical conclusion.

"Well, may I at least see the facility in case an opening becomes available? We could keep checking back to see when you have space." The lady in the doorway was not budging from her stance.

"Well, I wouldn't waste my time because we are full, and we will not have space anytime soon."

"Well, that's OK," I said, "I don't mind waiting, and I expect that we'll have other children, so I would like to see the facilities anyway."

I smiled sweetly at her obstinacy. I knew there was nothing about my exterior or mannerism to which she could object. I was professionally dressed, and I spoke with all the eloquence and confidence of a person with two higher education degrees. I had told her that we were homeowners in the area, and she could see that I was driving a late model vehicle. But yet, there she stood, refusing to engage with me any further.

A few seconds passed. She shifted her weight from one leg to the other, exhaled in frustration with my persistence, but could not think quickly enough to come up with another excuse. So she stood to the side.

"Well, this is it," she said as she waved her arm in one huge circle around the entirety of the room while she kept her eyes focused on me to make sure I did not cross the threshold.

I made a point of looking slowly around the interior of the brightly lit and well-resourced room, and then I took one step back and prepared to leave.

"Well, thank you for showing it to me," I commented after the 10-second tour, "but I do have one question," and looked beyond her glassy stare to hit my target.

"Do you have any black children who attend this daycare?

Check and mate. I waited for her reply.

"Well, um… we don't, umm, I don't…ummm."

"Never mind," I said. "I don't think that this is the right place for my child. Thank you for your time." I retreated to my car. I replayed the scene over and over in my head as I drove the three minutes to my house. Then I sat in the driveway and sobbed.

After that experience, I felt the need to shield my children from this kind of small-town bigotry. And though the private schools my children attended while they were growing up were primarily white, they had an articulated goal of diversity, and they welcomed my children.

After this horrible experience with the local church daycare, I found a beautiful Montessori school that I absolutely loved. I do not even know how the idea of putting my daughter in Montessori school came to me; I think I had been reading about it. As with anything else when I have to figure something out, I started doing research and somehow, maybe through friends, I found out about this school. When I went to talk to the staff, I fell in love with the whole concept, the whole idea of it.

But it was not my intention to send my kids to private school all of their lives, because I was always a public school girl. Right? And Tim pretty much left that decision to me because I had the stronger opinion about it. After kindergarten in Montessori school, I had to think about elementary school. There is an elementary school maybe a half-mile from my house. I pass it every day on my way to work. That is how convenient and close it is. I went to look at it and made an appointment to talk to the teachers and to the principal, and here is what turned me off. In the Montessori schools, my daughter Rozalia was doing very well. She was hitting all her markers, and the Montessori people encouraged independence and self-reliance. Rather than lining all the children up to go to the bathroom one after the other, they allowed the children to go whenever the need arose. That was part of that being "in tune" with one's self. And my daughter is like that; she is in tune with her own feelings.

After I made an appointment to visit the nearby elementary school, the teacher was taking me through the ropes. She proudly explained to me that "by the end of the first grade, they will know their numbers one through 10, and they will know the alphabet." For me, that was a very low bar. So I asked, "What if a child comes to first grade and they can do all those things already?" She replied, "Well, we make sure everybody is at the same level by the end of the first year of school."

I know I stayed another 30 minutes, but I did not hear anything else she said. I knew that my child was not going to that school. So that was it. I had fallen in love with the Montessori methodology, and they had a program through sixth grade. So we kept our kids in Montessori school through sixth grade, and in private schools through high school.

To be clear, the choice of where to send our children to school was never about race—it was about my perception of the quality of my children's education. Most of the local public schools were white. So my decisions were definitely based on what I thought were matters of quality, equality, and fairness. I wanted to be clear that the stated mission of the schools would allow my children to thrive academically and not just survive.

The price of our concern for the quality of our children's education, though, meant that the "starter" home that my husband and I moved into—well, we're still in it 26 years later. So while a lot of my friends were able to move into what I consider nicer homes in more upscale neighborhoods, my husband and I are still in the same place, a three-bedroom brick ranch. We made the decision to invest tens of thousands of dollars into private school education, and because of that decision, we were not able to move into the type of house I would have loved to have later in my career.

Both my children are smart and have been academically successful throughout school, including college, but so are lots of children who attended the local public schools. The high school dropout rate for black teens in our state remains too high, and the lack of access to gifted programs for black children remains too limited. So were we smart to live where we do and send them to private school, or should I have moved to another school district to send them to public schools? I try not to dwell too much on that question.

I must admit that I did think about the lack of racial diversity in the schools the children attended. I remember meeting with one of the teachers in Rozalia's preschool classroom. They were telling us all about the school. There was nothing I did not like about what they were saying, and I felt that it was a very natural decision to put her there. It felt like the kind of place that I would have liked to go to school. So the last question I remember asking was, "What is the diversity like in the school? I do not see many kids of color here, you know, black kids, here." And she said—this was such a perfect response in my mind—she said, "Well, yes, you are right. That is one of the things we want to work on, getting more black kids in the school and Hispanic kids, but you have to remember, LaHoma, that creating a diverse environment for your child goes beyond the school grounds, so we like to emphasize with the parents that it is important who they go to school with, but it is also important who they socialize with after school and who they go to church with on Sunday and who their parents are friends with." That was the perfect response for a person like me. She got me. There is only so much the school can do. If I send my kids to school in this environment, and for the other 18 hours of their day they live in a very different way, then that is not as effective as if there is consistency across all parts of their lives. That teacher's response and my beliefs tie into what Cindy said earlier: that she did not use the school system as the sole socialization mechanism, as the only organizing framework for how she raised her kids.

The degree to which we had our kids involved with afterschool activities, who their friends were, who our friends were—all that is also where I put a lot of time and energy in with my children. I wanted to make sure that they were getting a very well integrated community. So that is why I went to two churches on Sunday. My family is black; Tim's family is white. Our kids are just comfortable wherever. And in addition to all that, they were in an academic environment where they were thriving. I also put a lot of legwork into Girl Scouts and sports clubs and all those things where racial lines were more blurred, where there was a greater diversity of kids.

I am proud of what I see and hear from my children on racial issues. They have friends, and they date whomever they please, based on personality preferences, not race. My daughter developed this strong sense of identity at an early age. I will never forget the day she overheard her black camp counselors teasing each other about liking a white boy at school—emphasis on the fact that he was white. The camp coordinator later shared with me that Rozalia had asked the girls, "What's wrong with dating a white guy? My daddy is white." Embarrassed, the girls had no reply for her. She has continued to challenge prejudice and ignorance through high school and college, and it will be interesting to watch how she manages as she begins her professional work life. My son, who never understood my desire to discuss race at all because it never seemed like a big deal to him, has more recently tried to draw me into such conversations. He, along with the rest of the country, has witnessed via social media the tragic death of Trayvon Martin and other young black men his age. Now that he is close to college graduation, he seems to be paying closer attention to these issues, like it or not, as he makes his own way through school and beyond.

Our time together working on this book project has revealed where I have placed my time, energy, and resources: making sure that my children saw their place in a world that was welcoming to all, boldly embracing, and beautifully diverse. I look forward to continuing this same work with the generation to come.

EPILOGUE

What Now?

The desire for desegregated schools was about two goals: teaching children of different races how to live together and ensuring that black students had access to the same resources as white students. School desegregation was part of the path to achieving Martin Luther King Jr.'s "beloved community," an ideal manifestation of the inter-relatedness of all human beings regardless of the color of their skin, their faith, their gender or their wealth—a community of love and a community of justice.

Court-ordered desegregation actually moved us closer to that vision, according to research on school integration during the 1970s and '80s (12). In spite of this, the political will was not sustainable, and white parents found ways to resist by moving or sending their children to private schools and by voting judges out of office. Court orders were eventually almost all reversed. In the absence of laws to mandate desegregation, schools are once again highly segregated, with more than 70 percent of black students going to majority non-white schools and nearly 40 percent of black students going to hyper-segregated schools. Those students pay the price in lower school achievement and employment prospects (13).

Without court-ordered mandates, entrenched racial housing segregation continues to drive school segregation. Housing segregation is itself driven by a long history of racist policies— redlining and unfair mortgage loan practices, for example— that are not likely to change quickly. Court-ordered school desegregation did not work, and it will never be retried. There is no political will for such unpopular policy.

In the absence of courageous national leadership, creating the beloved community will require community solutions. But the communities surrounding hyper-segregated schools face multiple challenges with few resources. School districts need dialogue between and across communities and racial lines.

What if each school district were asked to come up with a plan for making the beloved community a reality, and what if funding became dependent on achieving that goal? This scenario sounds dreamy, but school systems spend a lot of money trying to fix what is wrong in an already broken system. What if they start with a vision of what they want?

Local decision-making for schools requires community-driven processes to figure out how to make racial equity work across a school district or state. It requires many people talking to one another to understand what their individual and mutual needs are. Community-based participation is not an easy process. It takes a long time, and it is frustrating to many people, because during the conversation it seems as if nothing is happening. The process makes funders and administrators nervous because it requires different metrics for success than are usually used; the process is difficult to manage and hard to evaluate in the short term. It takes political will and financial support to make community-driven solutions to racial equity in schools work. Stakeholders (parents, teachers, school administrators) who are not motivated to seek racial equity for its own sake will require convincing that racial inequities have costs for everyone (14).

Dramatic demographic changes in the South since we were in school in the 1960s and '70s will bring even more complexity to the task of locally driven solutions. The racial composition of schools is no longer primarily black and white; Latino children now comprise nearly the same proportion of students as black children do. In 1970 in the South, 67 percent of students were white; 27 percent were black; 6 percent were Latino, and less than 1 percent were Asian. In 2014, these proportions had shifted to 43 percent white, 27 percent Latino, 24 percent black and 3 percent Asian. Working toward racial diversity and equity within school systems where there are substantial percentages of white, black and Latino students will require that those participating in the efforts pay attention to multiple cultural understandings and requirements. (15)

* * *

There are no quick fixes, no silver bullets. There will be different solutions for different communities. Progress may mean greater racial integration, or it may not. Though we are talking about the need for non-white students to have access to all educational opportunities that white students have access to, we still want to consider the importance of keeping some safe spaces for minority students. Some students will benefit by having teachers of the same race who better understand their cultural context and who can challenge them without sending them out into the deep waters before they are ready. The resources at their schools must be equal to those at schools with majority white students, however.

Finding ways to achieve racial equity in public schools, as well as in all other institutions in our country, requires that people—black, brown, and white—find a way to talk to one another about the reality of race in their lives. Over the course of the writing of this book, our focus has been working together to find our truths about the role of race in our school lives. It was through our conversations that our most valuable insights occurred.

* * *

There are so many people NOT talking about race even as their beliefs about race direct their actions; they are uncomfortable talking about it, they do not know how to talk about it, and they need role models and safe spaces. Unfortunately not talking about race leads to more feelings of discomfort and distrust of people with whom we share no stories, no laughs, and no insights into each other's lives.

We, LaHoma and Cindy, ask you, the readers of this book, to think with us about the value of public school integration even in the absence of court-ordered mandates. We are not advocating the desegregation of our resegregated schools as scholars, or politicians, but rather as two people, one black, one white, who lived through, survived, thrived in, and reaped value from an experience that transformed our lives. We are people who came to understand the importance of creating a fair and inclusive society, one that benefits from equal and just access for all of its members.

Our hope is that our stories will encourage you to think about your own stories related to race, stories that have shaped what you believe or how you live your lives today. We hope that you will share these thoughts with others. And if you have friends of other races, we hope that you will share your stories with them, and listen to theirs, and together, begin a conversation. Through this dialogue, we hope you gain a greater understanding of how each of you feels about being a member of your own race. We hope you begin to understand the perspectives of people from races other than your own, and to see why something may seem threatening racially when it may not be about race at all. We hope that from these conversations, you can find your shared concerns, and that rather than putting up barriers, you will find a way to talk through the discomfort, face down your fears and find hope for the beloved community—together.

NOTES

Opening Quotes

hooks, b. (1996). *Bone Black: Memories of Girlhood.* NY: Henry Holt & Co., p. xv.

Alexander, E. (2010). Amistad, Cinque Redux. *Crave Radiance: New and Selected Poems: 1990-2010*, Minneapolis, MN: Graywolf Press, p. 212.

Obama, B. January 10, 2017, Farewell speech.

Chapter One

1. Barnett, N. February 15, 2015. Editorial, *News and Observer*, Raleigh, NC.

2. The increase in hypersegregation in the South and West since a 1991 low of around 26 percent reflects the effects of reversals of court-ordered desegregation. The percentages of black students in the Northeast in hypersegregated schools has been stable at around 50 percent since 1991, indicating lower initial levels of desegregation. See Table 8 and Figure 3 in Orfield, G., Frankenberg, E., Ee, J. & Kuscera, J. (2014). *Brown at 60: Great progress, a long retreat and an uncertain future.* A report. Los Angles, Calif.: The Civil Rights Project (UCLA); https://www.civilrightsproject.ucla.edu/research/k-12-education/integration-and-diversity/brown-at-60-great-progress-a-long-retreat-and-an-uncertain-future/Brown-at-60-051814.pdf

Chapter Two

3. http://museumofdurhamhistory.org/beneathourfeet/landmarks/WhittedSchool

4. Jackson, B. & Friedlein, K. June 17, 1970. "Unhappy Crowd Jams School for Desegregation Hearing: Some Support is Accorded Board's Plan." *Durham Morning Herald*, pp. 1A-2A.

Chapter Three

5. Comer, J. & Poussaint, A. (1992). *Raising Black Children: Two Leading Psychiatrists Confront the Educational, Social and Emotional Problems Facing Black Children*. NY: Plume.

6. Ironically, this new elementary school named after Mr. Harris was built with money raised from a bond he opposed on the grounds that it was being raised to build a school to perpetuate racism.

See   http://andjusticeforall.dconc.gov/gallery_images/ rencher-nicholas-r-n-harris-first-african-american-on-the-city-council-and-the-durham-county-board-of-education/ Chapter Six

7. Statistics found in Wheeler v. Durham City Board of Education, 379 F. Supp. 1352 (M.D.N.C.1974); http://law.justia. com/cases/federal/district-courts/FSupp/379/1352/1378164/

8. Cleaver, E. (1968). *Soul on Ice*. New York: Random House, Inc. p. 17

Chapter Eleven

9. Quotes by Dr. Lucas found in The Heritage Calendar 2017 website: Honoree--John Harding Lucas, Sr. Educator; http:// ncheritagecalendar.com/honorees/john-harding-lucas/

10. An excellent synthesis of the positive benefits of desegregation for black students is found in Appendix A of Orfield, G., Frankenberg, E., Ee, J. & Kuscera, J. (2014). *Brown at 60: Great progress, a long retreat and an uncertain future*. A report. Los Angles, CA: The Civil Rights Project

(UCLA); https://www.civilrightsproject.ucla.edu/research/k-12-education/integration-and-diversity/brown-at-60-great-progress-a-long-retreat-and-an-uncertain-future/Brown-at-60-051814.pdf

For research on long-term benefits of desegregation, see also Johnson, R. (2011). *Long-run impacts of school desegregation and school quality on adult attainments. NBER Working Paper Series: WP16664.* Cambridge, Mass.: National Bureau of Economic Research; http://socrates.berkeley.edu/~ruckerj/johnson_schooldesegregation_NBERw16664.pdf

11. Gershenson, S., Hart, C., Lindsay, C. & Papageorge, N. (March 2017) *The Long-Run Impacts of Same-Race Teachers,* IZA-DP 10630. Berlin, Germany: IZA Institute of Labor Economics. http://ftp.iza.org/dp10630.pdf

Epilogue

12. Court-ordered desegregation resulted in greater levels of desegregation, especially in the South, meaning greater resources for black students. Social scientists have demonstrated that when children in desegregated classrooms of all races had the opportunity to learn from and work with classmates from diverse backgrounds they showed improvements in critical thinking, a reduced willingness to accept racial stereotypes and a greater interest in cross-racial friendships.

See research summarized in Appendix A of Orfield, G., Frankenberg, E., Ee, J. & Kuscera, J. (2014). *Brown at 60: Great progress, a long retreat and an uncertain future. A report.* Los Angles, CA: The Civil Rights Project (UCLA). https://www.civilrightsproject.ucla.edu/research/k-12-education/integration-and-diversity/brown-at-60-great-progress-a-long-retreat-and-an-uncertain-future/Brown-at-60-051814.pdf

13. See Table 2 in Orfield, G., Kuscera, J. & Siegel-Hawley, G. (2012). *E Pluribus Separation: Deepening double segregation for more students. A report.* Los Angles, CA: The Civil Rights Project (UCLA); http://escholarship.org/uc/item/8g58m2v9

14. The negative effects of segregation on minority students such as lower achievement, higher rates of dropout, incarceration, poverty, poorer health status and job opportunities have real costs to our economy as well as our identity as a land of opportunity for all.

See Orfield, G. & Chungmei, L. (2005). *Why segregation matters: Poverty and educational inequality. A report.* Los Angles, CA: The Civil Rights Project (UCLA); http:// escholarship.org/uc/item/4xr8z4wb

See also introduction to Orfield, G., Kuscera, J. & and Siegel-Hawley, G. (2012). E *Pluribus Separation: Deepening double segregation for more students. A report.* Los Angles, Calif: The Civil Rights Project (UCLA); http://escholarship. org/uc/item/8g58m2v9

15. See Figure 1, p. 7. Frankenberg, E., Hawley, G., Ee, J. & Orfield, G. (2017). *Southern Schools: More than Half a Century after the Civil Rights Revolution.* Los Angeles, Calif.: The Civil Rights Project and Center for Education and Civil Rights.

ACKNOWLEDGMENTS

We are grateful for the support of friends and family during the more than three years we were writing this book. We want to give special thanks to Dr. Jane Brown who has been our teacher, our mentor and our friend, and who was present when we first conceived of it and has been a steady presence during this journey. We especially want to thank her for review and critique of a very early version that helped us focus and organize our narrative into what it is now. We also would like to thank Kate Torrey for an early read and useful comments and to Linda Brinson our line editor for asking us insightful questions and polishing up the prose.

We would like to thank Andre Vann, historian and archivist at North Carolina Central University, for his assistance with our research, locating important documents about the history of Hillside and about the court-ordered desegregation that happened in Durham City Schools. He was very generous with his time and his enthusiasm for this project.

We are so delighted to be publishing under the Torchflame imprint of Light Messages. We are happy to be publishing with a Durham-based press and be working with such lovely people, Betty, Elizabeth and Wally Turnbull and their publicist, Rebecca Schriner.

We'd like to thank Lucy Siegel for opening up her home to us last summer for a weekend writing retreat. We would also like to thank local establishments (Guglhupf Bakery, The Refectory, Caribou Coffee and Otis and Parker) for comfortable space—fortified by coffee, food, and wifi—that allowed for us to work together freely for hours at a time.

And of special note, we want to thank Dr. John H. Lucas Sr. for his kind words that opened this book and for his leadership as the principal at Hillside while we were there, in creating the school environment that made our experiences there what they were. He has lived a lifetime of service to the cause of equity in education and we are honored to have his blessings for this book.

LaHoma

I am indebted to my family for encouraging me to pursue the completion of this project. There were many days when I was not mentally or physically present because of my preoccupations with writing.

I am especially thankful to my husband Tim, who has been a rock solid presence in my life for 30 years and has helped carry me over every mountain I ever sought to climb.

To the Hillside Class of 1975 and other HHS alumni—I am proud to be among your ranks as graduates of our beloved alma mater. Thank you to all my "girls" (Angela, Cassandra, Debra, Dewanda, & Varnell; Cindy, we miss you, and Joyce, my girl, you left me way too soon) who have cheered me on through our regular get togethers and to all those who attended our class reunion in 2015, especially Bishop Daryl, for encouraging me to share these reflections with the wider community.

Lastly, to my co-author, Cindy, who, despite her own personal and professional transitions during this period, believed in and committed to this project and never waivered. Frankly, this book would have never happened without her. Cindy was the glue that sealed all the pieces in place. I appreciate her vast skillset, wit, vision, and creativity, which allowed us to successfully complete the task we started years ago. She is a woman of faith and courage, and we have forever solidified our bond as friends as well as fellow alums. Thank you Cindy for sharing this process with me.

Cindy

I would like to acknowledge the Center for Documentary Studies whose classes in creative non-fiction kickstarted my non-academic writing. A writing assignment in one of those classes was the initial inspiration for this book.

Thank you to all my family and friends who supported and encouraged me while I was working on this book project. Special thanks to Leigh and Sieger for sharing their lovely home with me on my visits to North Carolina to work on this book during the past two years. I want to thank my husband Ron Geary especially for literally making time and space for me to write this book. Thanks to my daughter Emily for helping me think through some of my stuck places and to my son Max for his interest in a possible stage play. Being their mother is a never-ending inspiration for me.

And finally, I thank my co-author LaHoma. My deepening friendship with LaHoma was the best part of sharing these memories. I was lucky to find myself collaborating with such a kind and gracious person, someone with a great sense of humor and with whom I shared so many beliefs and concerns about family and community. Because of my trust in her and our shared mission for this book, I was able to keep peeling back layers of memory to find some hard truths. I look forward to our continuing friendship and work on whatever opportunities arise from the publication of this book.

THE AUTHORS

LaHoma Smith Romocki

LaHoma Smith Romocki graduated from Hillside High School in 1975. She completed her undergraduate studies at Duke University and received both her masters and doctoral degrees in public health and mass communication at the University of North Carolina at Chapel Hill. In the '80s, she was a Peace Corps volunteer in the Central African Republic and recently completed a tour as Peace Corps Country Director in Cameroon, Central West Africa. LaHoma is currently an associate professor of Public Health Education at North Carolina Central University and has an appointment as an adjunct associate professor at the Gillings School of Global Public Health at UNC-CH. She lives in Granville County, N.C., with Tim, her husband of 30 years. They have two adult children, and her parents live close by, along with a large network of beloved family members.

Cindy Waszak Geary

Cindy Waszak Geary graduated from Hillside High School in 1973. She completed undergraduate and graduate degrees at the University of North Carolina at Chapel Hill and Northern Arizona University. She worked more than 30 years as a social scientist focused on global health, based in Chapel Hill, N.C., and traveling often to Africa and Asia as part of her job. She now lives in Baltimore, Md. with her husband Ron, where she consults for public health organizations, wrote much of this book, thinks a lot about racial justice, and enjoys more time for yoga. She is the mother of two grown children, and has one granddaughter. Cindy still considers North Carolina her home and returns frequently to visit her mother and friends.

Keep the Conversation Going

Learn more about *Going to School in Black and White* with LaHoma and Cindy at goingtoschoolinblackandwhite.com.

Follow Cindy and LaHoma at facebook.com/ goingtoschoolinblackandwhite.

Photographs and reading guide available online at:
torchflamebooks.com/geary-romocki
goingtoschoolinblackandwhite.com

If you liked

GOING TO SCHOOL IN BLACK AND WHITE

you might also enjoy these nonfiction titles from
Light Messages Publishing & Torchflame Books

Real Birth: Women Share Their Stories
Robin Greene

Faith and Air: The Miracle List
Scott Mason

Following the Red Bird: First Steps into a Life of Faith
Kate H. Rademacher

*Say to These Mountains:
A biography of faith and ministry in rural Haiti*
Elizabeth Turnbull

Raised by Strangers
Brooke Lynn